Share Your Mission

Volume #2

by

R. Winn Henderson, M.D.

**Contributing Authors: Steve Allen, Dr. Patch Adams,
Don Blue, Dr. Peter DeBeneditis, Dr. John Gray,
Mark Victor Hansen, Dr. Eric Kaplan, Brian Klemmer,
Dr. Carol Lieberman. Paul J. Meyer,
Dr. Joachim de Posoda, and Dr. Roberta Wilkins**

*Best Wishes and,
God Bless!
Win*

Share Your Mission: Volume #2

Share Your Mission: Volume #2

2001, R. Winn Henderson, M.D.

Library of Congress Cataloging in Publication Data

Published by:

Insight Publishing Company
P. O. Box 4189
Sevierville, TN 37864

Printed in USA
Cover Design: Feredonna and Douglas Graphics

ISBN No. 1-885640-76-5

Table of Contents

Foreword

What are the most prized treasures you can obtain in this life? Would they include a fancy car, a big bank account, a mansion on the hill, or a beautiful wife and family? No......*joy, happiness, and peace of mind,* are most people's greatest desires, but they can prove quite elusive and hard to obtain.

Short of actual experience, the most effective way to gain knowledge and understanding is by learning through the experiences of other people. **Share Your Mission** was created to help you obtain these spiritual qualities by exposing you to real life examples of other individuals with mission driven lives.

At the age of 30, Jesus began a three year mission as a preacher, teacher, and healer. Never before nor after has the world been so greatly influenced by any one person. Through miracles, parables, compassionate example, and ultimately through his own death, Jesus was able to instill in mankind a moral conscience and sympathy for the poor, the unloved, and the oppressed.

Though divine, Jesus chose to fulfill his mission through actual human experience. His example of service to others sets a precedent that far exceeds what we may ever hope to achieve during our lifetime, but personally, my greatest desire is to live life with the same enthusiasm for service that Jesus had for the welfare of mankind.

Share Your Mission: Volume #2

The radio talk show centers on the philosophy that everyone has a God-given purpose for being, a mission to preform in order to fulfill his or her destiny in life.

The talk show guests presented in this book bare their souls and give of themselves allowing the reader to share both the joy and the pain involved in discovering their missions in life. *Share Your Mission* shows how actually pursuing one's mission in life will open the doors that lead to the peace, joy, and happiness we are all seeking.

While I was interviewing the guests in this book for the radio program, I was impressed and challenged with their diversity of thought and the many sacrificial acts they endured to positively restructure their lives.

Their stories reaffirmed that most problems in our lives lead back to our unwillingness to grow spiritually. Our readers will thus be challenged by my guests to find a spiritual solution for any unhappiness they find in their lives.

The guests demonstrate that service to others is the common ground or key that magically unlocks all the potential goodness we each have inside us. By sharing our blessings with others we literally set ourselves free to fully live. Sharing allows us to reach out in compassion and love, and in return we are rewarded many times over.

Share Your Mission is dedicated to helping the listener or reader realize that he or she too has a personal mission in life. By sharing life experiences, we hope individuals will recognize and address their own personal need to reconnect with their creator, and seek His divine guidance in their spiritual journey.

Rich or poor, red, yellow, black or white, we are all precious in his sight. God does not play favorites. He gives everyone a mission to fulfill.

Share Your Mission — The Personal Thoughts of 12 Great Americans is a continuing series of books that we hope will enhance the efforts of these passionate individuals who are actively seeking to fulfill their destiny.

May God richly bless all your endeavors and guide you to a life filled with the peace, joy, love, and real happiness that you so richly deserve........

RWH

Life's Destiny

You are my father
I'm your son, your daughter
You're the mighty ocean
I'm a single drop of water

You're my creator
I came from you
To you I'll return
When this life is through

But 'till that day comes
I'll follow your plan
For I have a mission
And my mission is grand

I pray for your guidance
Your wisdom I seek
For without this knowledge
My life can not peak

Show me my purpose
My life's destiny
So I can be happy
So I can be free

Share Your Mission: Volume #2

Interview segments in this book are taken from the actual transcripts from the internationally syndicated radio talk show: **Share Your Mission** *which is funded by charitable donations of individual and corporate sponsors. Dr. R. Winn Henderson is the host and producer of* **Share Your Mission.** *Here's the introduction to the show:*

It's your life.
It's your destiny.
It's your choice.
And now it's time to
Share Your Mission.

Dr. Winn Henderson is the host of today's program... *Share Your Mission.* He is a medical doctor with over twenty years of clinical experience and the author of nine books including, *The Cure of Addiction, The Twelve Steps, Doctor's Don't Lie,* and *The Four Questions.* Dr. Henderson is the founder of the **Recovery Group** which counsels individuals and families with addictive behaviors, using a Christian based model, and of the **Destiny House** which is a spiritual retreat in the mountains of western North Carolina. **The Destiny House** provides an opportunity for individuals to find out **why** they were created and **what** is their mission i life.

Hello again..... this is Dr. Winn Henderson and the program is called **Share Your Mission.** Remember, the four important questions in life are:

Who am I?

Where did I come from?

What am I doing here?

Where am I going when I'm done?

Our program deals primarily with the third question:

What am I doing here?

I believe that each of us has a specific mission to accomplish, a destiny if you will, and the secret to finding true personal happiness in this life lies in discovering that destiny and then in pursuing it.

My mission is to help you find yours. I do that by teaching you how to love yourself and fully appre-ciate your value.

This is so important because until you fully appre-ciate and understand your relationship to God, other people, and the world, you will never be happy, content, or have peace of mind. And of course, the fastest way to gain that understanding is in answering the four questions.

The Four Questions, will help you find out **what** your mission is so that you too can be truly happy and successful. I want you to have a free copy of the book. To get more information, call 865-546-5537. We also provide individual Christian based counseling world-wide by telephone, and you can reach us at the same number, 865-546-5537. E-mail us at: *drhenderson@icx.net.* Our web site is *www.intl-speakers-network.com/rwhenderson* or *www.shareyourmission.com.*

John Gray

WH: Our guest today is Dr. John Gray. Dr. Gray is the author of the fabulously successful runaway hit, **Men Are From Mars, Women Are From Venus.** It was the #1 book on the USA Today's bestseller list between 1994 and 1998, selling over ten million copies. In the relationship field, it's a book that probably everybody has read, or at least heard about. **Men Are From Mars and Women Are From Venus** has transformed communication between the sexes and helped millions of couples worldwide. Dr. Gray has other books in the Mars and Venus series including: **Mars and Venus in the Bedroom, Mars and Venus in Love, Mars and Venus on a Date,** and **Mars and Venus Starting Over.** Now he has a new book which revolutionizes parenting. This book is called **Children Are From Heaven.** It's a compassionate, thoroughly modern guide to raising loving, happy, healthy children.

The world has changed dramatically in the past thirty years. We have drug use and violence reaching younger and younger into our families and our children. Clearly, the old ways of parenting don't work in today's vastly different society. But many parents make common mistakes, because they don't know a better way. Dr. Gray, with his trademark compassion and humor, shows parents how to abandon fear-based parenting with threats and punishment for a firm, but loving method, that allows greater com-munication between the child and parent.

From California today we have Dr. John Gray on the line. Dr. Gray, how are your doing?

JG: I'm doing great, thanks so much.

WH: To start off, please tell us about yourself, your background, and how you got to the point that you're at today.

JG: Briefly, I grew up in Texas. We were a Christian family. Back in the 60's lots of kids were taking drugs and so forth. I liked rock and roll and I wanted to get high as well, I but didn't want to take drugs, so my alternative at that time was transcendental meditation. I became part of the TM movement group for nine years. During that time, I became a Hindu monk. I lived a very spiritual lifestyle, although I was still Christian. I'm all religions, although my background is Christian. I'm very open to see the good in everyone.

Then I became a marriage counselor after nine years of being single and devoting my life to God, my spiritual quest, and mainly living up in the Swiss Alps. I came back into the world, started having relationships with women, because that was the message in my heart from God, that I was here to do something, not just to spend my life seeking heaven, finding oneness with God, and experiencing God. Rather it was to bring the *experience* of God and the love in my heart into the world and make a difference in the world.

I'm so honored to be on your show, which is about finding your mission in life. It was through my many, many years of prayer and meditation, that I was able to go inside my heart, for the motivation to come out into the world, find my mission, and to do what I'm good at. As it turned out, I was really good at counseling people. People would talk to me about their problems, and I listened and I counseled them.

Because I had been single and not in a relation-ship, when I started having relationships with women, it really did seem like women were from another planet. I knew myself as a man, and how I was, and how I thought, but to be with women was a new experience for me. But I came from a spiritual, loving perspective which was not to judge. I started to see that women were not the way men saw them. Men were not the way women saw them. Men and women were misinterpreting each other again and again. By clearing up a few common misinter-pretations, communication could improve. With better communication, relationships dramatically improved.

I've been doing this now for twenty years.......teaching this material. During this time, I had been doing research and teaching but yet hadn't written the book: *Children Are From Heaven.* The same principles I applied to adult relationships, I apply to parenting. We simply need to understand the uniqueness and differences between children, and understand what their needs are, instead of assuming we know what's best for them. We need to recognize that different children have different needs. Often, if you have a child that's not cooperating with you, it's because what they need is counter-instinctive to you. That means that what you would automatically give is what you would need. Your instincts say, "give what you would need."

The bible says, "Do unto others as you would have them do unto you." This is the underlying principle of love. Yet, at the same time, we have to generalize that statement, "Do unto others as you would have them do unto you." This means that you'd like other people to respect your needs, and you need to respect their needs. You cannot respect someone's needs unless you know what those needs are.

As parents, we mistakenly assume we know what our children's needs are. In the book I talk about four different types of children that have completely different needs. Then

I talk about the gender differences between children. Boys will need something different from girls. And, as an overall picture in the book, I talk about how children in this generation, some of the children in our last generation, and some of us when we were growing up, have been the early children in this category. These actually are a different kind of children than ever before in this world. We have different needs.

You might say, well, what do you mean by this? What I mean is, the world has changed so radically in the last 200 years with democratic government, with human rights, with freedom of speech, adults have changed, businesses have changed their practices of managing people, yet parents quite often, are still doing the same things their great grandparents did raising their children. We have to update and adjust our parenting skills, just as society has updated its way of dealing with people. Love has to be the basis for it. Violence is clearly not an expression of love, even when it's to protect ourselves.

I guess we do this because we don't know another way. But today we do have an alternative that works. We can be loving and we can learn to successfully communicate. This is my hope in the world. As most civilized people say, "We want a world of peace." This was a new idea that started in the 60's. We want a world of peace without the violence

This can really only start when we learn to raise our children without the violence.........without threats of punishment. I've found you can actually raise your children in a firm, strong way, and yet staying in tune with the old phrase, "Spare the rod, spoil the child." You have to have the rod, but certainly nobody beats their children with rods anymore, nor with switches. Now we're gradually starting to stop spanking them or trying to control them with threats of punishment. Most parents don't know what else to do. So they say, "How bad do they have to be before you punish them?" I explain, you don't ever have to punish them. You can learn other ways to manage your children so you never punish them. I learned this technique through my seminars for children.

I did seminars for children of broken homes...... children who were getting in trouble and about to go to jail. Almost all of them were already grounded for the rest of their lives, so I had no threats. I had no punishment to control them. I had to find another way. I found alternative ways. I learned a good idea from dog obedience training, which is: when you reward dogs, they change their behavior and successfully communicate. I looked at some of the communication skills between tiger trainers and tigers. That's how I felt when I was with these kids......... like I was in a cage with a bunch of tigers. How was I going to control them? I learned how to do it, and that's what I explain in this new book - ***Children Are From Heaven***. It's a way parents can stay congruent with the loving feelings they have towards their children all the time.

WH: We're talking today with Dr. John Gray. Dr. Gray's new book is – ***Children Are From Heaven.***

Dr. Gray, I want to go back for a second because I'm interested in this. Please tell us, what is a typical day in the life of a monk?

JG: On a typical day, you would wake up and bathe. You would then meditate for awhile and pray. Now this is not the Catholic monk. My affiliation at that time was with the transcendental meditation movement, and the founder of the transcendental meditation movement was Maharishi Meshiyogi, a fine person of the east, who's made a great impression on the world. I got very close to him, was actually his personal assistant, and lived with him for many years. I observed basically, his life style, and became a Hindu monk during this time.

My lifestyle was one of getting up, bathing, meditating, having a very small breakfast, maybe a little bit of fruit or just some tea, going back and meditating, doing exercises and praying for many, many hours, having a very small lunch, and then doing spiritual reading for several hours. I would also go for a walk in nature and come back and meditate for several hours, have a regulated dinner, a small dinner, getting together with others sometimes in the evening to read spiritual books, sing spiritual songs, or to discuss basic community life, in a very quiet sense.

Having times of silence....... For me particularly, I would spend one month at a time in silence each year. I would spend the first week of every year fasting on water in silence in a room the whole time. I would just pray to God every day and meditate for hours and hours. It was a beautiful, rich and rewarding life.

However, it wasn't the time just then to find my mission in life, I needed all of that to connect with, to feel within my heart, my connection to God. And I did experience very, very clearly, that beautiful connection to God, and I could then hear the voice of God motivate me in my life.

For me, the way I hear the voice of God is not as though somebody comes in and says, "John, today you ought to do this." It's more that when my heart is open, filled with love and devotion, I feel a yearning in my soul to do something. The first thing I felt a yearning for, was to do something different from this.

I've loved this journey. I've loved this path, but I had to go to go back to the world I came from. I had to go to back to America. I had to go back into the world, into relationships, into being a responsible member in the community. I felt a little bit like a hypocrite, giving advice to people and being spiritual when I wasn't raising kids, facing the daily challenges, paying mortgages, going to work, dealing with bosses, dealing with paying bills.

So from that perspective, I went out into the world to be an example of what I wanted to teach people, instead of just having holy thoughts and ideas. I wanted to first go live those ideas, to see what was possible and to see how it was possible, and then share those ideas. That's what I've done in my life, and that's how I found my mission. I continue to stay in tune with mission in this life by listening to my heart.

When I'm really in touch with my feelings, when my heart is really open, I ask God, "What am I here to do? Show me the way." Always a feeling comes..... or the question is just in my mind, and then some-thing happens that day or the next day. I read something. I hear something. It just clicks and it just says, "Yes, that is it."

Another way God speaks to me........He can speak to me through my children. He can speak to me through a client. He can speak to me through a verse I read in the Bible.

He can speak to me through a phrase in a book I read or somebody I talk to, or by watching the news. Something just comes to me, and if I have the question in my heart, I go.....that's it, that's what I want to do, or that's the answer to my question. So that's the way God speaks to me, through my heart and through other people.

WH: I think that *where* we're at in the world at any particular time, is the result of every good, or bad, or neutral experience that we've had up until that point of time, and that people who have had unusual experiences or what they consider bad experiences, shouldn't feel bad about them necessarily, because they wouldn't be where they're at, if they didn't go through those experiences. I don't think that I could have been a monk for any length of time, but I think that in your life, you wouldn't be where you are today if it hadn't been for going through that experience.

JG: Clearly, that served me enormously and I want to just reinforce the message that you just gave, which is that all of the life experiences that we have, whether they be good or bad, all have something to teach us on our journey in this world. If we don't learn the lesson, and we don't see them as in some way as teachers, or in some way an assistance to our mission and our growth, then we tend to keep repeating similar kinds of experiences until we're able to learn from them. That's just a simple piece of logic. If you make a mistake and you don't know it's a mistake, you'll keep repeating it.

Flip that around. Something comes to you and it's a lesson, but it didn't feel very good. If you don't learn a lesson from it, and you say, "I don't want that to happen again." It keeps happening again and again, until you learn the lesson from it and then it doesn't need to happen again.

Clearly, I see people wandering around their lives wondering why their life isn't what they want it to be. They say, "I'm a spiritual person. I'm a good person. I'm doing the best I can. Why is it not happening for me?" There's a variety of reasons, but one common reason for that is, that in some of our interactions, we haven't learned the lessons we're here to learn.

One of the big lessons that all of us are here in this world to learn, is the lesson of forgiveness and responsibility. When we feel responsible for something, it's hard for us to forgive ourselves. If it was bad or a problem, or if somebody else is bad or a problem to us and they're responsible for our misery, they're responsible for our suffering, they're responsible for our discomfort in life, we tend to not forgive them. We tend to grumble about that person or still feel hurt by that person. When we do that, we're giving away our power to create our life the way we want it to be. We're giving that person power over us. We're saying that, yes, my life isn't completely the way I want it to be because of what that person did to me. Instead of saying, "That particular day, was not the way I wanted it to be because of what that person did, but tomorrow's another day, and I have the freedom to create my life the way I want it to be and the power to do that comes from my relationship with God." That is the whole secret to creating the life that you want, not just a loving relationship with God, but a relationship of prayer......where you feel your heart opening to God. You feel a connection to God and then you ask God for help.

One of the problems that I see so much in society, is that people only pray and ask for help when they're in dire need of help, when their life is desperate, when they're dying on the battlefield, when their loved one is in danger of dying. Then they beg God for help. They open up and say, "Please help me." At other times they think God is too busy to share their needs and requests. So they don't have a day-to-day relationship with God, when God is there to help at all times.

God is infinite, omnipresent, omnipotent, capable of taking care of everyone of His children at any time. All we have to do is ask. And that is the rule, that is the guidance. *You must ask.* If you don't ask, you don't get. That's very,

very important.

When my children were very young, they didn't have to ask, I took care of them. But as they get older, I needed to start giving them more freedom to do things on their own, and they wanted to do things on their own. However, when they needed help, they needed to ask. Then I give them help. That's an important part of growing up....... learning how to ask for help, how to ask for assistance, how to ask for support in an effective way.

An important relationship skill, particularly for women, that I teach in my books, but also men, is to learn how to ask. Many women have to be motivated to ask. Men generally are already motivated to ask. Instinctively, women have to be taught. That's alright. You have the right to ask. You should ask. It's a good thing to ask, and if you don't ask, probably he's not going to know that you have a need.

God may know all our needs, but God lets us ask. We have free will, which means, we have the will to do it ourselves. We have the will to do whatever we want, and if we have the will to receive support, that support is always available to us. It doesn't just come. You can't take God for granted. Every day you've got to ask for that help.

I start every day asking for guidance, asking for help,

asking for support. I say, "This is what I want to happen, would you help make this happen?"

This is my little prayer that I do. You know, this is for me personal, but I'd like to share it. You can adopt this prayer, and it can help to encourage you to use your own prayers. But mine is......

"Oh God, my heart is open to you.
Please, come sit in my heart.
Use me today to bless this world.
Use me today to make this world a better place.
Please God, give me wisdom, give me direction.
Give me the confidence.
Give me joy.
Give me more opportunities.
Give me the right words to say, so that in this interview,
I'll say the perfect things so that people will be helped."

And that way, I don't have to do it all myself. As many Christians who pray will say, once they feel that connection, that support, that the anxiety leaves their heart, because they're not alone.

Depression and anxiety, two most common sufferings that

society has today, is when we feel we have to do this by ourselves. We forget that we have a partner in life and that God is always there. It just appears sometimes as though God is not there, if we're not asking for that support on a regular basis.

WH: You're so right about that. When I was practicing medicine, before I retired, I think a good 35% of the people that came through the door to see me were either suffering from anxiety or depression. They had an empty feeling, a feeling of impending doom, and they were nervous about it.

However, that feeling goes away when you have the proper connection with God, you allow the Lord to live in your life, and to help you and guide you. The whole difference in whether you're healthy or not healthy, I believe, depends on your understanding of your relationship with God.....and in applying it.

JG: You bring up the term, healthy. This, in my mind, relates a lot to the theme of this show, which is finding your mission in life..... achieving your mission in life. When you're in tune with your mission in this world, your purpose, what you're supposed to be doing here.......when you're doing what you're supposed to be doing here, you tend to be very healthy. When you're not doing your mission, you tend to start getting sick.

Use it or lose it. If you're not doing what you're supposed to be doing, then the true self starts to wither away and your body starts to get sick. Not that there's not other causes of sickness. There certainly are, but I believe this is one of the foundations of health, particularly for those of us as we get older.

There's this thought that we're supposed to get sick. We see people getting sick all around us, and we feel that old age means getting sick. Old age doesn't mean getting sick. There are many cultures even today, certainly not in the civilized world, but in the more indigenous areas, where people live in the mountains and they don't have all the stress. They work every day and live to be 100 to 150 years old. Women can even bear children at 100 years of age in some cultures in this world today. But they don't have the stress that we have to encounter. *What* they are doing, keeps them peaceful. They know their mission.

WH: John, would you tell me specifically.....what your mission is?

JG: My mission in life, is to love, and be of service, to both myself and to others around me, to my family and friends, and to the community at large.
My specialty in that process is to help couples love each other more, help them to raise healthy, cooperative,

happy children with great self-esteem and confidence, to teach people how to have a loving and healthy relationship with their body so they can live a long life and be strong, healthy, and vibrant, and to create a loving relationship with community as well.

I feel that as any person gets older and older, their needs in service changes. In the beginning, it's more about serving ourselves, then our spouses, then our children, then the community, and then as we get over into our 50s and 60s, it's more about serving the world and helping everyone. In this way, we build a basis for love throughout our lives and we create a more loving world.

WH: That's a wonderful expression of mission and purpose. I wish you the best of success with the rest of your life, Dr. Gray. You're making a very meaningful contribution to the world. Thank you so much for being on the program today.

JG: You're very welcome, thank you.

Share Your Mission: Volume #2

Steve Allen

WH: Our guest today is Steve Allen, and I'm going to do his biography.   It's quite an extensive biography.....listen to this......In the twenties, thirties and forties the single most talented individual in the entertainment world was Noel Coward who achieved great success as an actor, vocalist, pianist, author, composer, lyricist,   and director.   During a visit to our shores in the early fifties, Sir Noel described Steve Allen as the most talented man in America.

Andy Williams once said, "Steve Allen does so many things, he's the only man I know who's listed on every one of the yellow pages."

It is in fact, difficult to believe that there is only one Steve Allen.   He is the only TV comedian from the golden age of comedy in the fifties who is still appearing frequently on TV.

He created and was the original host of the *Tonight Show.* He's written   54   books......one of which we're going to be talking about today.

He starred on Broadway in   *The Pink Elephant*   and in motion pictures, most notably   *The Benny Goodman Story.* He's written   over   8,600   songs   and   scores   for   several musicals.   He's made 54 record albums or CD's.   He's written an Irish drama, *The Wake*.   He starred in the critically acclaimed ABC series, *The Steve Allen Comedy Hour.* He's created,   written   and   hosted   the   Emmy   award-winning PBS TV series   *Meeting of Minds.* and he has been inducted into the TV Academy's Hall of Fame.

Not bad!......Hi Steve, how are you doing?

SA: After listening to that recitation, I'm exhausted.

WH: Only your mother could have done better.

I forgot to tell you, he's married to the actress-comedian Jayne Meadows. That's very impor-tant too.

Steve, your book is called **Dumbth....The Lost Art of Thinking With 101 Ways to Reason Better and Improve Your Mind.** Your theory is that we, as a society, are getting dumber by the day.

SA: I wish it were only theory, and I would be happy to have it disproved. Unfortunately, it's all too well documented. There's no one who differs with the thesis once they understand what we're talking about. The American people are getting dumber.

Whenever one who has access to public attention, learns about a problem, there's something within us that wants to take charge of the situation, to the extent that one person can, do something constructive or helpful about it. So I've been working on that for a great many years, and this book is only one of the results of my concern about the collapse of intelligence.

You were kind enough to mention the *Meeting of Minds*

program. That's another example. Then there's a record album I did for children about 30 odd years ago called *How To Think*. There are other instances too, but we don't have time to list them all. It is really the ability to think, in other words, to achieve what the human race has that distinguishes us from all the other millions of creatures that share the planet with us. It would be a shame, for example, if we said, "Well the class of creatures called birds are the only ones that can fly," and then we found out they hardly ever fly. Well, we're the only ones that can think but so many of us hardly ever do any real thinking. We do a very basic sort of thought that even infants are capable of, such as, where's dinner?, or, I'm hot, let's go to a colder place, or something of that sort. But that's not what we talk about when we use the word "thinking."

WH: Why is it that we're getting dumber? Are we just lazy or is it something other than that?

SA: There's a long list of causative factors. The problem is like another that's so heated right now, about the degree of violence, vulgarity and general shock and sleaze in television, films, and recordings. Some people point in one direction, some point in another, but we should be pointing in all relevant directions because in both of these cases the list of causative factors is very long. Some of them are not so obvious. For example, the American people have been involved with several major wars during the last century, and even though we were fortunate that none of them were fought on our soil, war always has destructive effects on the civilian community as well. Obviously, it does for young men who have to do the fighting. Sometimes daddy goes away and never comes home, or he comes home with only one leg. Men who showed great promise, who were deprived of their families, either never returned home except in a body bag or returned greatly handicapped from what they suffered in war. So in that sense then, the fabric of families back home is torn and frayed, and that never does any good for a society.

Also on the list of people or institutions that should be blamed is as we were discussing a moment ago the popular media. Television apparently is concen-trating so much on ratings and it's learned that by pandering to human weaknesses, and sometimes depraved human appetites, you can round up a few more listeners or viewers. Some of the people who own TV stations, networks, and production studios, who before this point, seemed to be decent enough citizens, are perhaps now revealing their true moral colors in that they will sell anything if there's an audience for it, in which case they are no morally better than those who are in the prostitution, heroin, or the cocaine business. So we're talking about very deep moral questions which of course, have impact in the economic structure of our society.

WH: It would seem to me that the 102nd way to better improve your mind would be to turn off the television.

SA: It would be a good thing to do, depending of course on what you did instead of watching television. If you just went down to the bowling alley or the neighborhood saloon, then I doubt if turning off TV would do it for you. It all depends on what use you make of television. If there were some dictatorial individual or system of government which could totally control television, television would get marvelous the next day.

I'm not recommending dictatorship. That always leads to other problems that we don't want either. But the point is, there is marvelous stuff on television. There are programs like *60 Minutes, 20/20,* and *Dateline,* which are a fine use of the medium. There was a brilliant two-hour production just a few nights ago, of *Law and Order,* which dealt with the Russian Mafia and its impact on America's large cities. That too, was an admirable use of television.

You just watch the *History Channel, PBS,* and that sort of thing, and the better shows, you can learn a lot from TV. It would be a pity to give that up. But unfortunately, the reality is, especially as regards ratings, is that often it's the most depraved, sickening, and vulgar shows that have big ratings. So one would naturally walk away from that kind of television.

WH: Out of your ***Dumbth....The Lost Art of Thinking With 101 Reasons for Ways to Better Improve Your Mind,*** what's the number one reason in your opinion?

SA: I don't think, that one of them deserves to be rated number one, which would mean that it's regarded somehow better than all the others. They all are of importance. They're not necessarily of equal importance.

For example, to deal with a specific rather than an abstraction, one of the ways in which young people in our country are incredibly ignorant..... because to be ignorant in the abstract is almost a meaningless statement.....you have to be ignorant about something that other people do know. And it turns out that many young Americans are incredibly ignorant about simple geography. Now, I mention the word 'simple' because even scholars can't answer all questions about world geography.

I remember I was watching a newscast one evening a few years ago when I was writing *Dumbth*, and it had a feature that dealt with the degree of information possessed by members of a geography class, not in fifth grade, but at the University of Miami in Florida. The degree of ignorance on the part of these 19 and 20-year-old people was shocking, even to me, and I'm familiar with general ignorance that prevails. I don't have time here to review all the statistics but they're in the book. I'll give you just one. Eight percent of those college students did not know where Miami was, and they were in it! That's pretty scary!

As a matter of fact my friend Jay Leno, who hosts the Tonight Show as you know, does an old routine of mine where he takes a camera out on the street and puts very simple questions to people. He called my office the other night and wanted me to see one of these shows. I watched it, and it was incredible what people don't know! The scary thing is, is that it's what 10 year old Americans used to know 30 or 40 years back. That shows how far we've fallen from our former state, and we were never all Rhodes scholars to begin with.

WH: I thought it was kind of funny........this weekend my wife and I were out "yard saleing" and we were trying to find a yard sale on Boright street.   We passed a fellow who was having his own sale, so we stopped and asked him, and he says, "Well I think it's somewhere around here.   I'm not exactly sure."   So we said, "Okay,"   turned left,   and Boright was one street away from him.

If you don't even know the name of the next street away from the one   you live on,   how are you going to tackle some of the really tough problems in the world?

SA: You're exactly right.   If I had heard about that one before, it would have been in my book.   Some of the stories now add up to comedy because comedy is about tragedy. There are lovely, beautiful things in life but we never joke about them.   We joke about all the negatives, the wars, the disasters, the diseases, the divorces, all the bad things.

If you want an example of "dumbth", a friend of mine, the late comedian, Alan Sherman, whose parodies were brilliant, because of the   big sales in records for him,   was some years back, the number one comedian in the country....... for at least a few months!   So he was on tour, and you know if you're traveling a lot,   it's hard to keep up with your laundry.   So he arrived at a nice hotel in St. Louis with a plastic bag filled with about six soiled shirts that he needed to have laundered and returned to him promptly.   When he checked in, he put the bag of shirts up on the counter in the hotel, and said to the manager, "I'm leaving, as you probably know, Thursday morning, and I have to have these shirts back by that time, okay?"

The manager assured him that he would personally see to it, and a couple of days later Alan was checking out. He said to the manager, "Oh, by the way, what about the shirts?" Now the man reaches down under the counter, pulls up the same bag of still filthy shirts, and says, "Here they are Mr. Sherman, just as promised."

That is a classic instance of what I call "dumbth". It may add up to a funny story now but some of the instances of dumbth have catastrophic circumstances. Airplanes crash. Buses drive off hillsides. There's all kinds of really sad results from this kind of poor thinking.

WH: Which would you rather be......stupid or ignorant?

SA: (Laughter) My mind has never made much profit out of those rhetorical choices. Just like the old debate about 25 years ago, would you rather be dead or red? Fortunately, we're not in a position where we have to make any choice. Back then the thing to try to do was avoid being both red or dead. Let's not get trapped in rhetorical questions.

WH: If a person reads your book, how is he likely to improve his way of thinking?

SA: It'll improve a person in 101 ways. First of all, some of it will affect his supply of knowledge. It'll affect his ignorance. But there are a lot of instances where warning signs in the book will steer him away from muddled thinking.

For example, not many people know that we are all biased. Generally they will speak critically of bias. They'll say, "Oh, he's very biased on this question, or don't waste your time arguing with her, she's biased." It's important to know that everybody on earth is biased. But as long as you do know that, it's a little bit of self-protection in that you won't argue quite so dogmatically. You're perfectly free to give a well reasoned presentation of your case, but it makes us all more humble and a little more charitable in a debate with other well-intentioned people whose opinions are contradictory to our own.

So there's no way you can go on and still be dumb if you absorb those 101 lessons, which is of course, the reason the book is selling so well.

Teachers love it, for obvious reasons, because it refers to thinking. It refers to studying and learning. There are three or four teachers I have met in the past year or so who have told me that they made the book required reading for their students.

WH: I believe that there are many ideas and many concepts that if people would be aware of them, and would embrace them that the world would be a better place. Unfortunately, it seems that in spite of the fact that great things have been written, most of the people just don't care.

SA: That's exactly one of the aspects of "dumbth". I don't think there could be such a thing as a person who would read this book and at the end of it, decide that he just didn't care. But you're absolutely right. There are people who, we've all heard that sarcastic expression.....need to get a life.

There are some people whose lives are so narrow, so selfish, yet sometimes they may have an excuse. Maybe they've never had much of an education. Maybe they've had a very bad example in the home in which they grew up. So it's not that we should run all of these people out of town because they're not as smart as somebody else.

But for people to *stay* deliberately dumb when it's not necessary for them to do so, is another matter.

As an example of dumb, I mentioned somewhere in the book....... imagine what would happen if Dan Rather went on the news tonight and announced in all seriousness, that it had been discovered in a scientific study, and was being announced now by the Federal government, that eating bananas is a strong contributor to cancer.

We know what that would do to the banana fruit industry. Bananas in the stores would rot and companies would go out of business. It would have widespread marketplace consequences. Fortunately, I'm talking about something imaginary. There's no such problem in reality. But again, if there were such an announcement, it would kill that particular market, the banana market.

Now let's turn to reality. We know that over 400,000 Americans......it's up now to about 425,000 Americans every year are dying from inhaling tobacco smoke. That is a simple scientific fact. The people of the tobacco industry lied about it for some years, but they finally were disgraced and exposed, and at least they've stopped lying, which is some kind of moral progress. Now every American teenager must have heard all about this. It's been in the papers, on radio, and on television. It's been discussed in schools. It's been mentioned in movies. You can't get away from this message, that *tobacco causes cancer.*

So you say, what's that got to do with "dumbth"?

I'll tell you. A lot of young people, despite all this knowledge, are deciding to smoke anyway, after all the lessons, after all the warnings from the White House and from Republicans and the Democrats and from the churches and from doctors, from all the people who know what they're talking about. When a young person today says, "Oh, to hell with it, I'm going to smoke anyway," that is a classic example of capital D, "Dumbth"!

WH: How right you are!

Now the third question that we talked about earlier, "What am I doing here", related exactly to what you just said. If a person has a mission in life, if they have a destiny,

29

something that they feel that's very necessary for them to do before they die, and they're focused on that, they can't in good conscience do the kind of things that they know is going to shorten their lives and give them less of a chance of fulfilling that mission.

SA: You're right. I'm very lucky in that I have about 47 missions. Unfortunately, since I'm now 77, I'm not going to live long enough to do adequate justice to all of them. But it has always seemed since my own childhood, important to educate myself, because we all start as total knowledgeless "dodos".

A baby doesn't know anything. It's adorable but doesn't know anything. It has to be taught everything. Eventually, a few instinctual abilities click in, but we all start with a blank slate. And, for some reason or other, even when I was just six years old, the importance of education was always clear to me. In modest ways I would try to help some of my buddies who were in school with me, and I've never stopped that. I'm still speaking at colleges and high schools, writing books, doing television work and that sort of thing, all on the theme of education.

Just to give another example.....I didn't volunteer for this particular work, but was asked to do it, and I willingly accepted the invitation. I am a very lucky survivor of cancer, and I realized about 16 years back when I had that experience, that the fact that I had survived it could be inspiring to others. It could give hope to a lot of people, because the word cancer itself brings fear, and understandably, because it kills millions. In the old days it was simply a death sentence. They didn't do anything about cancer. Now they can do a lot about it, particularly if it's discovered early. So that's another thing that both Jane, my wife, and I do as a matter of fact. As both survivors of cancer we willingly speak, lecture, and write articles, just to share our experience with others. As I say, it can give them hope and some courage.

WH: I think that your mission in life can change many, many times and whatever it is.... whatever you feel your mission is now, is the correct one. Of all the things that you've done in the past and up until now, things that you're doing right now, what do you see as your primary mission?

I mean, what is the most important to you if you had to limit it to one thing, what would it be?

SA: I tend to resist the temptation to limit any of my interests to one solitary item. However, it's an easy question to answer, if the judging factor is, what am I spending the most time at.......to what activity am I devoting most of my energy.

And again that is the nationwide campaign against the vulgarity, violence, coarseness, and ugliness of so much of popular entertainment. I'm affiliated with an organization called the *Parent's Television Council*. There are many organizations active in this campaign.
One of them is the old Catholic group, *The Christophers*. Their approach has always been to reward the good and the virtuous and hope, by holding them up as examples of the

31

better worth, to place the emphasis on the better and discourage or de-emphasize the negative and the evil.

There's a group called *Morality In Media,* based in New York, which is active in this campaign. There's a group called the *Dove Foundation,* which puts a seal of approval on video cassettes of motion pictures when they're okay for the family to see. So, in answer to your question, the thing I'm devoting most of my time to now, is this campaign. I've written a number of articles about it and am constantly speaking on the issue and I'm glad to report that the message is finally getting attention here in the Hollywood production centers. They finally are beginning to understand they are doing something wrong and that the American people want it stopped.

WH: If someone listening to you today wants to get involved in this, is there a number that they can call to get the specifics?

SA: As regards *The Parents Television Council*, here is an address: P.O. Box 7802, Burbank, CA 91510.

WH: What advice would you have for a young person coming up today when peer pressure teaches him or her to be dumb?

SA: One of the things I would do is endorse your own idea, Doctor. In fact the point is, in a certain way, mentioned in my book. I put it this way.......try to get interested in other people a little more or at least as much as you're interested in yourself. Do some work on behalf of others, for which you don't expect a reward. If you get one, that's nice, but most of the heroic work in this world hardly ever gets any particular reward, certainly not a monetary one. And often the hero goes to his or her grave unknown, even to the immediate culture or society in which he does his fine work.

WH: That's great advice. Service to others has to be one of the most fulfilling things a person can do.

SA: Do you know that even in the scriptures where Jesus is quoted as referring to the classic virtues of faith, hope and charity, He puts charity first. Think of that! Most people probably would put faith first, forgetting His teaching. But when the question was put to Him, He gave them a great answer. And the beauty of that is, that it applies to everybody. Even if there were no God, or even if you're talking to 14 people who don't believe in God, they too can do wonderful charitable work. However since there is a God..... then you could say, "Even without knowing it, they're doing God's work."

WH: How true!

We're talking with Steve Allen today. His new book is called *Dumbth: The Lost Art of Thinking and 101 Ways to Reason Better and Improve Your Mind*. It's an important book that you need to read. For more information about my friend, Steve Allen, you can visit his web site @ www.steveallen.com.

I want to thank Steve for being on the program today. He's told us a number of things that are very important and crucial. We really appreciate it, Steve.

SA: Thank you, Dr. Henderson. It's been a pleasure to talk to you and your many listeners. Thanks so much.

Editor's Note:
In October Steve Allen departed this world for a better place. We are sorry that he didn't get to see this final interview about the things he so passionately was involved in changing for the better.

Carol Lieberman

WH: Do you think that there's too much violence on television these days? Well, there's a lot of people who do and think that's it's really hurting our children and us as we become adults. Our guest today is Dr. Carol Lieberman. Dr. Lieberman is a psychiatrist from Southern California. She's is also a clinical professor of psychiatry at UCLA and a diplomat of the American Board of Psychiatry and Neurology. She is a media consultant and has done lots of different things with respect to the television industry. We're going to have her talk about that in just a moment.

Carol, you're with us today in California. It's early out there but we're pleased to have you with us and we'll be talking about an extremely important topic today, I think something that you're passionate about.

CL: Absolutely!

WH: Tell us about your professional career and what you've done and where you're at right now.

CL: I went to medical school at the University of Luzanne in Belgium and learned medicine in French, which was an interesting challenge. I did some internships and then did my psychiatry residency at N.Y.U. Bellevue, which was an incredible place, because really we saw all kinds of psychiatric problems. You know, from people who hadn't gotten treatment in years and were very sick, to people who wanted psychoanalysis for sort of what's called the "worried well". Then I came to California after my psychiatry residency because I wanted to work in the entertainment industry in order to be able to share the insights that I got about mental health with a larger audience.

In other words, I always knew that I didn't just want to sit in my office forty hours a week and see one patient after the other, because even if I did that for years, it would still limit the number of people that I could help. I wanted to work in television and radio, and by consulting two television shows and movies to try to either directly help people by talking to them myself or trying to make sure that what people see in the movies and television shows are accurate because people really do get, mostly unconsciously, their information about what they think other people think and feel through watching movies and television shows.

WH: You're the script consultant for **The Bold and the Beautiful** and **The Young and the Restless**. In that respect, you tell them what's going on with respect to various different types of psychological problems of the characters in the shows, right?

CL: Yes. I read all the scripts every week and make some comments and suggest some future story lines based upon what the characters are doing now and if there's anything that seems out of character or is medically wrong. A lot of times there are various medical illnesses that the characters get then I write notes about that and they correct it.

Now they're very responsible, actually they're the only soap operas who have an on-staff consultant, (psychiatric consultant) and they're wonderful to work with. There are people who don't think they need to have a psychiatric consultant because they don't really care unfortunately whether it's accurate or not. Actually, it's a little more complex than that I mean, there are a lot of people in Hollywood who, unfortunately, don't care. They just care about making a lot of money with their products. But there are people who are overwhelmed by the idea that their movie or their television show could actually have an impact on people. You know, it could change somebody else's life. Part of why they don't want to get help for that or don't want to think about that too much is because it's just overwhelming to them, because they don't really know how these things happen.

It's been interesting over the years in an area that I've really been particularly interested in......the phenomenon of copy-cat behavior. We've seen it particularly in copy-cat crime like all the people who copied *Natural Born Killers* and went out on rampages and killed people in that same way or *Scream*.......the scream movies. There have been some crimes copying that. *Fatal Attraction*, that wasn't per se a crime, I guess in a way it was a crime, that idea of pursuing, stalking. It was interesting how, after that movie, men and women began stalking each other more. So I'm fascinated by, and want to try to explain to other people and want to try to stop these kinds of bad behaviors of copycatting before they begin.

WH: What percentage of the producers out there in Hollywood are socially responsible as opposed to the ones who just want money?

CL: It's a small percentage. I don't know exactly but it's a small percentage.

What happens is, that people come out here and some people get a hit, if they're a writer or an actor or producer. Some of them eventually make it obviously, and in one project. And then they develop a lifestyle that has a huge mortgage and other huge expenses and they find themselves taking pretty much, whatever comes along in order to keep up their lifestyle. That's when people stop thinking about what's best for the universe and just what's best for them. That's very sad.

WH: Sounds like they prostitute their values to keep up with the power, greed, and that kind of thing.

CL: Yes. It's very difficult. It's difficult to keep your direction when you get on that track. We see examples frequently and we're going to be seeing even more. The envelope keeps getting pushed every year with some of these shows that are coming up. In **Survivor** for example, people are going to be on a desert island. The winner gets a million dollars......he is the one who survives. It's supposed to be rather dangerous.

Who wants to marry a millionaire? No one forces those people to do it, but it's just sad that we have gotten so cynical about love, romance, and marriage.

I've written a book called ***Bad Boys.....Why We Love Them, How to Live With Them, and When to Leave Them***. It addresses the idea that so many women are......The women on that show for example, I am sure, were hurt by many bad boys, guys who cheated on them, lied to them, and they just thought, I'm not going to get Mr. Prince Charming the normal way. Why not try to get married and particularly to a millionaire?

WH: I want to talk about ***Bad Boys*** here in a minute.
Let me ask you. You're a great outspoken leader against violence in the media, you're co-founder of **HOPE**, which is Hollywood Organizes for Positive Entertainment, and as the past chairman of the national coalition on television violence, I think that most of us feel like there's too much violence of television. Would you speak to the fact of where your research and your experience has led you with respect to the violence and what it's doing to our society?

CL: Violence in our society and in the media is a very frustrating situation. It's one that I haven't given up on trying to solve, but the research shows and has shown for years, that people, adults and children, watch violent television shows, violent movies, play with violent video games, play with war toys, guns and things like that, listen to violent music, any kind of medium where there's violence. If someone is exposed to that, they become desensitized to violence and they become more aggressive themselves and it's cumulative. The more violent media someone is exposed to, the more aggressive or violent they become.

It's kind of like the tobacco industry where they kept saying, (despite all the reports that cigarettes are causing cancer,) that it wasn't true.....not that they had anything concrete to point to show that it wasn't true. They just kept denying it. That's kind of where we are now in Hollywood. Now I've been working on this, trying to get people here to cut out the violence from the media products for over a decade. The progress that I've seen and to which I have testified before congress, stopped the Schwarzenegger rocket of which I'll tell you about in a minute, I've protested outside movie theaters. I've done everything. The progress that's been made in the past decade is that at least people now realize, acknowledge that violent media does cause people to become aggressive. But the problem is that nobody's doing very much about it. They're not doing much about it as far as making these products. There's still lots of violent media. It's gone up and down. When we have been protesting the most it goes down for a little while, but then actually when that's happened (since around 1993,) the sex on television increased, because sex and violence sells. It's all so unfortunate, but some people who do realize that now There were a lot of surveys after the Columbine incident where people were asked.......what do they think caused this.....contributed to this? People did realize that it's a combination of the parents not raising them in a loving household, obviously something being missing, either abuse or neglect going on and exposure to a lot of violent media. We know that those two boys were exposed to a lot of violent media on the Internet and other places. The polls show that the general public realizes not just for their situation, but in general, that there is too much violent media and that it's causing violence.

However, this is the same public that's buying millions or billions of dollars worth of video games and war toys, records or CDS, and video tapes and all the violent products. So even parents are not really following what they now are increasingly realizing to be true.......that the violent media does cause their children......people say well not my children, but it is the case. What's unfortunate is that a lot of times parents buy things for their children, violent media products, because they want to empower their children and they're afraid that if everybody else is watching these things, they want their child to be as tough as the next child.

It's very sad. It's a question of people feeling powerless all over the world and wanting to try to do something to empower themselves and their children. However power shouldn't be the same thing as violence.

WH: Well it's a catch-22 type situation with the media and the public going back and forth. I feel that all of the bad things in the world are a result of somebody's fear, and if we could somehow get rid of fear in general, on an individual basis or on a wider basis, we would have a wholly different planet to live on.

CL: Yes, I feel that's true. Let me just tell you briefly my Schwarzenegger rocket story.

WH: Great! Go ahead.

CL: This is one of those things that I'm most proud of having accomplished. In 1993, I read in the LA Times one morning that there was going to be an NASA rocket being sent up. I don't know if you've heard of this, but it was going to be sent up and it was going to have on the outside of it an ad for Arnold Schwarzenegger's next movie which was *The Last Action Hero*. I heard that and thought I was in twilight zone because I couldn't believe first of all, that there would be any kind of ad on the side of a NASA rocket, but no less, a violent one. Here's the first ad that would be advertising violence.

So I started a campaign that lasted three or four months. I went around the clock doing interviews until three o'clock in the morning, whatever time anybody wanted to do it all over the world, different time zones, to get people to call or write or fax or somehow communicate with NASA. I gave out this NASA hotline or the president of the United States or the president of Columbia or Sony. That was who was sponsoring the movie, Columbia/Sony. Apparently, these people got flooded with faxes or phone calls and the idea was, I was calling on people to express their displeasure at this happening. What ultimately happened was......there was a sort of time pressure because the rocket was supposed to go off in three or four months after the article was in, and so I had to keep trying to gather signatures........gather people complaining in enough of a quantity to stop it. And in fact, ultimately they did. It actually stopped the rocket.....which is not necessarily what I wanted but it stopped the ad.

What ultimately happened was that the people......it was partially funded by private industry for their experiment to go up on the rocket.....because this was getting so much negative publicity, television shows, print, radio, everything, Donahue, all kinds of shows........the people who were supposed to be connected with it, the private industry, pulled out because it was such a public relations nightmare. They didn't want anyone knowing that they were supporting this when there was obviously so much of a public outcry against it.

WH: Well this is a good example of why, when someone says, "There's something wrong here...... someone needs to do something about it......" It's quite often that that's the person that needs to do something. And you did. That's great!

Let's talk about your book, ***Bad Boys.*** In this book, you talk about attraction of women to twelve different kinds of bad boys, and you say that quite often the problem lies with the relationship that a woman has with her father when she's growing up. Can you tell us some more about ***Bad Boys***?

CL: Yes. The kind of relationship that a little girl has with her father as she's growing up sets a model in her mind for what will happen with men later on. So if a little girl has a father who abandoned her or was a workaholic or was a wimp and let her mother make all the decisions or cheated on her mother or whatever. There are twelve different kinds of scenarios that I describe as to how this relationship can cause the girl to consciously or most likely unconsciously pick a man who either is like her father, or the opposite of her father, or is in some other way affected by this.

I'll give you an example. I illustrate each of the twelve types of bad boys with fairy tale examples to start off, so that people can understand right away what the guy is like.

One of the examples would be Beauty and the Beast. Beauty didn't like the beast at the beginning and was very upset being there. With time she did finally change her mind, felt attracted to him, and went back to him when he was lying in a cage needing to be rescued. That fits with what her relationship with her father had been because her father.....when the story begins.........had lost his wife, her mother, and his fortune.

Beauty loved her father very much and he loved her, but her father was very sad and throughout her childhood, Beauty wanted to make her father happier, to rescue her father. Of course, as a little girl she couldn't really correct the things that were wrong with his life and so she felt as though she kept trying to rescue him and it wasn't working. When the beast finally needed her to rescue him and she was able to do that, that's what turned it around and made him seem like the man for her.

WH: Well, in **Bad Boys**, you have twelve different scenarios of different types of relationships that women get into that aren't good for them. You explain each of these in the book. That book is available at bookstores, and on Amazon.com I would assume?

CL: Yes.

WH: Okay, great! Let's talk about your radio talk show. You do a radio talk show, don't you? It's called *Media On Your Mind.*

CL: Yes. Actually, I have been doing that in LA for several years. It's been on hiatus for a few months but it's going to be starting up again. That takes my same interest in analyzing the media and applying that to psychological issues. What I do on the show is take a movie, a current movie, and interview the people from the movie, the writers or the producers or actors, a combination of some people from the movie, with real people who are undergoing that kind of experience in real life. Then we talk about that and have people call in to talk about it some more, either to talk about the movie or to talk about how these issues relate to their own lives. Usually I pick movies for that which have some kind of psychological or sociological significance, whether it's about truth or whether it's about some kind of illness or some romantic situation. It's the story that I use as a jumping-off point for people to really discuss this issue in their own lives.

WH: That sounds like a great show. One of your competitors, if you will, Dr. Laura, has a show. What do you think about her philosophy?

CL: Oh my........We've had some public scuffles,   not physical ones,   but I used to write a column and it was called **Hollywood On The Couch**.   Each week I would analyze a different news maker, a celebrity.   I didn't really get to pick who it was,   the editors did that.   Then I would do a background search on that person.   Really you spend a lot of time digging into their childhood and history,   and then come up with sort of a mini psychoanalysis of them and explain whatever problem they were having at the time.

With Dr. Laura,   I called her a menace to society,   and then I explained it and supported why.

Basically,   it's because she's perpetrating a fraud.   She's not a   psychiatrist   or   a   psychologist.   Her   doctorate   is   in physiology.   She   has   an   MFCC   degree   in   therapy   which is......you don't have to study many years to get that.

What concerned me about her is how,   first of all...... her answers to the questions that people.....I listened to know what was going on, but I can't listen to it,   because it's like chalk on a blackboard.   She tells people things that are so wrong but really they come out of her own childhood,   the unresolved issues in her own childhood that cause her to get angry or nasty towards people, because it's really bringing up something unconsciously in her own mind that she doesn't want to deal with so she reacts to people that way. I think the   reason   why   she   has   been   as   successful   as   she   has been.....well it's a couple of things,   but one reason is the public does have a thirst for trying to understand themselves and that's all fine.   I think sometimes.......it's familiar to too many people ......this kind of abusive, parental figure.

Listening to somebody else get abused, in a sense, is comforting to people who have come from an abusive background themselves. They can sort of identify with the person being abused, but it's not healthy at all.

WH: It gets back to that same thing of the public wanting to see violence, sex, abuse on one hand, and then on the other hand saying that's it's not a good thing. It's a double standard.

CL: Right. I think it's a very unfortunate kind of thing. I think that if people realized more why they were doing what they were doing they wouldn't be as likely to do it. That's one of those missions they have to try to get people in touch with their unconscious, with their vulnerabilities, with what's really going on so that they can share their vulnerabilities and not do things to cover them up....not have quick fixes to cover them up.

WH: You started to talk about your mission. Is there more to it that you want to tell us about, what your goal in life is right now?

CL: I think my mission or missions in life have to do with allowing people to express themselves and be cherished for who they are and understand what kinds of problems they have and how to get over these problems and to not be hurt.....to sort of preserve the little child in them.....and to not have that child's eyes glaze over or get clouded over with some of the painful things in the world but to somehow be able to understand what's going on around them and how to block them rather than to cover their child self up.

WH: That's wonderful, Carol.

We're talking today with Dr. Carol Lieberman. Dr. Lieberman is a psychiatrist from Southern California, and we've had a delightful time talking with her for the last thirty minutes. I know that some of the things that she's had to talk about today will be very helpful to you as you continue to think about them. Carol, thanks for being on the program today.

CL: Thank you.

Joachim de Posada

WH: Our guest today is Dr. Joachim de Posada.   He is a doctor of psychology and an adjunct professor at the University of Miami.   Dr. Posada is bilingual and speaks fluently in English and Spanish.   He has been conducting sales and management training programs worldwide for Fortune 500 companies for many years and is a featured television and radio speaker on the Human Factor in Business and Sports. He has co-authored three books, "Anthology of Great Speakers", "Where the Heart is: Stories of Home and Family" and "Celebrate Selling: The Consultative Relationship Way". He has produced four videos in English and two in Spanish. One of them, "How to Survive Among Piranhas," is a best seller in Latin America.

He has been a consultant in Sports Psychology for the Milwaukee Bucks and the Los Angeles Lakers of the NBA as well as Olympic athletes and teams in various sports.

Hello, Dr. de Posada, tell our audience about yourself a little bit more than what I did and hit the highlights of what you think is really important.

DP: I was born in Havana, Cuba and came to this country when I was 13 years old.   My dad put me and my 11-year-old sister on a plane headed for the United States because he wanted us to live in a free country.   I didn't know at the time why they were sending us to the U.S or what he had in his mind when he said that we had the right to be free and not live under communism, but it all made sense later on in time. Luckily, my parents were able to join us a few months later. We went from very rich in Cuba to very poor in the U.S; but we were free and freedom has no price.

While going to school, I started delivering newspapers in the morning in order to help my parents. That was one of the things that made me realize the ethics of work and how hard it was to make money. I went to middle school and then to high school in Coral Gables but I received an offer for a scholarship to play basketball in a school in San Juan, Puerto Rico and off we went. I graduated from High School in San Juan and went to undergraduate and graduate school there. While I went to school, I needed some extra money for expenses and got a part time job as an entertainer in Night Clubs. I was a stage hypnotist! Lots of people ask me why my name is spelled Joachim instead of the Spanish version, Joaquin. This is the reason.....I needed a more mystical name so I thought that Joaquin spelled in German sounded different and made it more mysterious. The name stuck and I never changed it back to Joaquin.

While working in Night Clubs and doing Seminars on Hypnosis, I got interested in the power of the mind so I started studying psychology and human behavior. Why was it that some people were successful and some were not? What were the characteristics of winners and losers? Why do some persevere and some give up very soon? Why do some people reach their goals and some don't even have goals? Nature or nurture? This is how I developed my passion in life. .....the search for truth. Then I developed my mission in life to help people develop their skills, change their attitudes, understand their potential, make a difference and leave a legacy.

This work has taken me across the world to more than 30 countries and has allowed me to meet very interesting and successful people everywhere.

Having played basketball, I took this knowledge into the sports world, and shortly after I started helping athletes, 27 years ago, I met Del Harris and worked with him and his team, and we won the Puerto Rico basketball championship. We have maintained a great friendship, and he has given me the opportunity to work with the Milwaukee Bucks and then the Los Angeles Lakers.

I just came back from the Olympics in Sydney, Australia and was able to help many athletes there, and it was a wonderful experience. I am very impressed with Australia and Australians. They are wonderful people, and I recommend everyone to visit Australia.

WH: You have talked about success.....so what does success mean to you personally?

DP: That is a very profound question. To me success means achieving happiness. If you do not do what makes you happy, if you do not express your passion or find your mission in life, your happiness will be limited, and maybe I should say, wasted. I think that Abraham Maslow had it right when he said, "The deepest level of motivation is self-realization." When you realize that you are making a difference and that what you are doing has meaning for yourself and for other people, you are well on your way to a happy and fulfilling life.

WH: Would you say that to a great extent that success can be equated to or measured in terms of how much service you give to other people?

DP: I would say that success is in a great part, what you give to others. This myth about equating success to making money, or possessing material things is just that, a myth. I understand that success has to be defined by each person individually, but for me, being healthy, finding love, loving your family, fulfilling your mission in life, helping others help themselves, and leaving a legacy......that to me is success and happiness.

WH: You said that when you were 13, you came to this country, and at that time you really didn't have a good appreciation for freedom. After you have been here all these years and have traveled to many different countries around the world, what's the difference between the United States with respect to the freedom that it gives its citizens, and their ability to be successful as a result of that freedom, and the other countries to which you've traveled?

DP: I have had the opportunity to travel all over the world and I truly appreciate the greatness of this, my adopted country. Don't get me wrong, there are great countries all over the world, most are free and those that are not free are not so great because they don't enjoy freedom. I can think of Cuba, Vietnam, North Korea, Libya, Iraq, China and I am sure there are others.

Let me give you a recent example. I just returned from Colombia where I filmed my latest video that will be out in February. It is a country rich in natural resources, rich in human resources and yet it is going through a very difficult period in its history, economically and politically. There are communist guerrillas that want to take over the country drug dealers, there are kidnappings, and there are daily killings. People every day look at the newspaper to read how many were killed the night before. The day I left, 14 were killed. I cry for Colombia and for all my dear friends that live in that country.

What can be done to help them? Well, the U.S. can help, and the Organization of American States can help, and even the United Nations can help, but it is a difficult situation. I believe that what is most needed is a leader that will rise to the occasion and gain the trust of the people.

Remember, 20% of the citizens cause 80% of the problems, so whoever takes control has to focus on eliminating that cancer that is affecting the country. This is a difficult situation indeed, but I am optimist, and I know that one great Colombian will rise and do something about it.

Cuba is another example. A country that has been destroyed by a repressive dictatorship of more than 40 years and its people are suffering because of this lack of freedom, lack of opportunities, and lack of basic human rights that we take for granted in our country.

In the States, we are very fortunate because our ancestors in 1776, Ben Franklin, Thomas Jefferson, and George Washington had a vision of what they wanted the country to be. I truly think that the drafting of our Constitution by these great men was a very important factor in the development of this great nation.

You know, as I traveled all over the world people would ask me if we were worried in the States about the situation that arose in electing our President, and I would tell everyone that there was absolutely nothing to worry about because we had a Constitution that everyone respects, and laws that everyone follows ......that we would soon have a President that would take over the reins of the Nation.

I was right. We now have a President that will guide this nation for the next four years and I wish him the best. Our Constitution is a big reason why we are successful. There are countries that have had twenty-five constitutions over the last three hundred years, but we have had only one and in over 200 years, it has had only 26 amendments to it, reflecting changing conditions, but keeping the core of it intact.

Yes, Dr Henderson, I sincerely believe that the success of this great Nation in great part must be attributed to our forefathers!

WH: Let me ask you a question: As individuals progress in life, they are quite often successful based on, in some part, the people they run into and the conversations they have with them.   Another way of talking about this, is talking about mentors.

In your life, have you had some mentors that you can tell us about that have affected you and influenced you and how they did that?

DP: I have been very fortunate to have met great people. I have had breakfast with Margaret Thatcher, I have met Presidents of many countries, I have been to the White House and have met our last four Presidents, I have met authors, entrepreneurs, company presidents, star athletes, ordinary decent honest people, fathers, mothers, housewives etc.   If I were to pick some of the most influential people in my life, the list would be too long for this interview.

My father, I would have to say is the most influential person in my life, and I could give you dozens of reasons and lessons he taught me all through my life. If you want me to tell you about someone not related to me, I will mention Steve Allen. I am so honored to be in this book with him. Steve Allen taught me a very important lesson in my life. He and I were having dinner one night and he said to me that "if we wanted to progress in humanity and if we really wanted to work for progress, we had to teach children how to be rational thinkers."   He took out of his pocket a cassette that he had done for 6 and 7 year old kids and I took it home with me, and when I heard it I understood that he was aiming at children to teach them how to think, teach them how to be smarter and he was looking at children as a way to better humanity! Instead of being worried about all the stuff about being old, he was thinking about our youth and how to make them more successful.

The other thing he taught me.....he said, "In order for you to be successful in life, you have to be funny! You have to use humor. Everyone is born with the ability to be funny." That lesson, I have always applied and I have tried to be funny and humorous in my speaking because people relate to it! People feel happy with it and that is an important thing I have learned from Steve Allen.

WH: Steve Allen certainly was one of the funniest men I know, and talk about creativity, I can't imagine being able to create as many things as he did in his lifetime.

DP: Yes, Steve Allen was "Mr. Creativity" in person.

You know Dr. Henderson, reflecting on this question, I met another   person that has made quite an impact on my life. I was attending a conference in Dallas a few years ago and when I looked at the program, a name caught my attention. That name was Arum Gandhi. I immediately looked at the bibliography to see if he was related to the great Mahatma Gandhi and I found out that he was his Grandfather. The following day, I looked all over for Arum and when I found him, I said to him "Mr. Gandhi, my name is Dr. Posada, what a pleasure to meet you. I have been an admirer of your grandfather all my life. He was such a wonderful leader, and did so much for man-kind." You must be so proud to be his Grandson! Arum said, "Thank you so much, yes my grandfather was a great man, I have always admired him." I said to him, "Mr. Gandhi, could you tell me about a lesson you learned from him, something that has served you well all your life that I can share with my audiences all over the world? He said, "I learned many lessons from my Grandfather. My father sent me to live with him when I was 12 years old until I was 13 and a half".

He started telling me some lessons he had learned from his Grandfather, but suddenly, I noticed a gleam in his eyes and he said, "You know, I learned a very important lesson from my father that I will never forget". Please tell me about it, I said.

He went on to say that he was 18 years old and his father asked him to please take him to work the following day in the morning and then to take the car to the repair shop to have it fixed. Next morning when they got to the office building where his Dad was going to be attending an all day meeting, his Dad told him to take the car to the shop and wait until they repaired it and then come back and pick him up at exactly 5 PM. He specifically told him not to be late because he was very tired and he was going to have a very long day and he wanted to get home early. Arum said, "ok," and off he went to take the car to the shop. At noon, Arum got up to go out to have some lunch, when the mechanic came out and said the car had been fixed and handed him the keys. Five hours, 18 years old, and a car, is a bad combination. Arum left with the car and started riding all over town. He finally found a theater and went in to see a couple of movies. When the movies were over, he looked at his watch and it was 6:05PM. He jumped from his seat, went to his car and drove very rapidly to the office building where his Dad was waiting for him.

There he was, his Dad standing in that corner with all the traffic, noise and typical warm weather in India, patiently waiting. Arum got out of the car and handed him the keys and said, "Dad, I am so sorry, for being late". His father said, "Son, what happened to you, I have been so worried" Arum said, "Those damn mechanics Dad, they couldn't find what was wrong with the car!" Arum didn't know that his dad had, at 5:30PM, being very worried, gone inside the building to call the repair shop to find out what had happened to his son. They had told him that the car had been repaired and that the son had left at noon.

So, at that moment, his father knew that his son was lying. I ask people in my seminars, when I tell this story, what do they do to their kid in a situation like this when they know that the kid is lying? I get all kinds of answers from slapping him, to pushing him inside the car, to taking him home and taking away privileges, being grounded, etc. Here I am, sitting in front of this gentleman from India and in my paradigm of India, discipline etc, I am waiting for him to tell me that his father took him home, hanged him from the ceiling, whipped him, then had the neighbors whip him etc. So, when I asked Arum, "What did your dad do to you?" I was shocked with the answer and it taught me one of the most important lessons in my life. He said that his dad handed him the keys and said, "Son, go home in the car because I have to walk home." Arum said "Dad, walk home, 15 kilometers, why?" His Dad replied, "Because I have to punish myself for being such a bad father and I have to meditate on why I failed you as a father.

If in 18 years, I have not been able to earn your trust, I have failed as a father. I apologize for being such a bad father and from now on, I will try to be a better one."

I was stunned. I asked him "What did you do?" He said that his Dad started walking, and he got in the car and drove next to him and started pleading with him to get into the car and he wouldn't do it. He walked with Arum next to him in the car for five and a half hours until they finally got home.

I asked Arum, "What did you learn from your Dad that day?" He answered, "I have never lied to another human being again!" What a lesson. You have to look within first before you blame everyone else. That has been one of the most important lessons I have ever learned in my life.

WH: I think that is a wonderful illustration and that taking personal responsibility before blaming somebody else is the way we really need to act.   It is amazing the amount of intelligence in that decision to approach it in that way.

DP: Exactly. If I have time to give you one more...... I once saw Larry Bird, a couple of hours before the game, bouncing a ball from one side of the court to the other. He was going at it very slowly, looking at the floor. I asked him what he was doing and he said that he was looking at every inch of the court because courts have defects or places where a ball might bounce irregularly and he could lose control of the ball. If his team was winning by 1 point with 5 seconds left or losing by 1 point, he could not afford to lose control of the ball.

I was left speechless. Then I understood. If you ask Larry Bird to jump, he would have been #250, or run he would have been #197, or do anything else, he wouldn't have been number one in anything, yet, his willingness to do things that other people were not willing to do, made him one of the best basketball players in history.

The lesson here is: ***Successful people are willing to do things that unsuccessful people are not willing to do***. If you want to succeed in life, you have to do things that other people aren't willing to do.

WH: Those are some wonderful stories. Let me ask you specifically.....in your life, what is your mission?

DP: My mission is to be a force for positive change and to inspire others to be the best they can be. I will strive to be a catalyst for action, for creativity, and for positive thinking. I will continually invent the future, looking out for opportunities rather than being a victim of the past. I will strive to choose my way, always seeking the truth, exercising courage, justice, kindness, understanding and personal integrity. I will constantly remind myself that without risk there is neither success nor failure. I will take an active role in being a good citizen and defending this great country, my adopted homeland. I will not forget my roots and will do anything I can to help my country of birth gain its freedom. I pledge myself to being the best dad in the world and a caring and honest friend to those around me.

I will be the best professional speaker I can be and will use the power of the platform to deliver powerful material that can change lives.

Finally, I will choose humor as a vehicle to make fun of adversity so as to help myself and others accept the good and the bad in life

WH: I have been working with people for the last 20 years who have psychological complaints....... nervousness, depression......as a result of bad things happening to them because of their addictive or compulsive behaviors. I have found they don't have a focus in life, or a mission, or something they can be passionate about every day. Therefore, they are bored, and they look around the world for things to make them feel better about themselves. As a result, they run into the things that are common and available like alcohol, drugs, controlling other people, over spending, and all the other kinds of addictive things that get you into trouble.

In your life, you have a specific mission, something to get up and look forward to every day. Would you agree with me that this is one of the primary things that keeps you from being distracted by all these other things that might make your life miserable?

DP: One hundred percent! I think that one way of helping those people is to help them find their mission. Help them find their passion in life. Give them something worthwhile that they will be willing to work for. Some people never find it! That is why we have so many people that are falling into addiction. I believe humans can beat any type of addictive behavior. We have a choice in life and those choices will produce good results or bad ones.

WH: We have been talking to Dr. Joachim de Posada. You can reach him at www.jdposada.com where you can check out the web site, and if you have any additional questions, you can e-mail him at JOACHIMNSA@aol.com. He will be glad to talk to you.

Thank you so much, Dr. de Posada for talking to us today, we have learned so much from you and we really appreciate the time you have taken to spend with us to help people with your good ideas.

DP: It was a pleasure to be on your program, Dr. Henderson.

Mark Victor Hansen

VH: Today's guest is Mark Victor Hansen. Mark is a professional speaker who, in more than two decades, has made over 4,000 presentations to more than two million people in 32 countries. His presentations cover sales excellence and strategies, personal empowerment and development, and how to triple your income and double your time off. Mark has spent a lifetime dedicated to his mission of making a profound and positive difference in people's lives. Throughout his career, he has inspired hundreds of thousands of people to create a more powerful and purposeful future for themselves, while stimulating the sale of billions of dollars worth of goods and services. Mark is also a prolific writer and is author of *Future Diary,* *How to Achieve Total Prosperity,* *and* *The Miracle of Tithing.* He is co-author of the fabulously successful series, *Chicken Soup For The Soul,* *Dare to Win, The Aladdin Factor,* *and* *The Master Motivator.* Mark has also produced a complete library of personal empowerment audio and video cassette programs that have enabled listeners to recognize and use their innate abilities in their business and personal lives. His message has made him a popular radio and television personality. Mark is a big man with a big heart and a spirit to match. He is an inspiration to all who hear him, and we're very pleased to have Mark with us today.

How are you doing?

MVH: I'm more than wonderful. That's almost too much introduction, Doctor Henderson.

WH: It's like when I go to speak and they give me an introduction, I say my mother couldn't have done it better.

MVH: Very lovely, thank you sir.

WH: Mark, this is a serious program in that we bring a serious message to many people. The message is that you are an important person..... you were created by God in God's image..... you have a purpose here on this planet..... and when you get through with your purpose you're going home to God. I believe that the way to get personal satisfaction in this life, is to discover what your mission is and then to pursue it. I know that you have a mission, and I'd like for you to share that with the people.

MVH: Doctor Winn, I agree with you at every level. The first one is that I think everyone of us is coded at birth with DNA and RNA, with a life assignment. I think mine is.... what we say with the *Chicken Soup* series, because it's sold 50 million books, is that we want to change the whole world, one story at a time from a Christian model.

When I was a kid, I learned the word "parable." It was said to be a story within a story, but now I really understand what that means. I thought it was something esoteric, far away, and something that only a theologian would understand. But now I've got it.

A little teenager came up to me and said, Mark, your stories are so good, they're "four noodle" stories. I said, "What's that?" He says, "So good I've got to tell my best friend, mom, dad, and even my dumb brother."

I'll tell you a joke, and I know you'll tell me one back. But if I tell you a story that really touches your heart and evokes your emotions..... like when I talked to 10,000 marines, they said, "We don't cry, but you made our eyeballs sweaty." We have that in the book. When you read a great parable, a great story, it evokes you to tell your story, and that's why our stuff works. That's why I think it absolutely fits your third question, **Where am I going?** What a story does, is to reconnect you with who you really are and how God is in you.

WH: I think that this is fantastic work that you're doing with the Chicken Soup series. Each book has 101 inspirational stories in them, and they cover all different types of life challenges, don't they?

MVH: Yes. We just got a letter from a prisoner who said, "Dear Mark and Jack, (I work with a partner, Dr. Jack Canfield), and he said, "I've been in the slammer for five years, contemplating the ideal crime.... killing the guy who put me here, and then my sister sent me one of your books and I've now read it six times. When I get out of here in five years I no longer want to kill the guy that put me here." And that's a pretty..... you know, being transformed by the self-renewing of your mind....that's a pretty good flip, wouldn't you say?

WH: Yes, I believe, if you can reach just one person, it's made your life worthwhile....and you're reaching millions.

MVH: The reason is that stories are the things that go from one heart to another faster than anything else. Everyone finds a story sort of irresistible. It gets inside you, it hits you at a visceral level, and it changes you.

I have to believe that Jesus was unequivocally the best storyteller. I don't know why it took 65 years for the Scribes to finally decide to lock it in and write it down. I'll bet His stories, when He was there were even better than what we've got. That may sound blasphemous. I don't mean it that way. What I mean is that the man had to be the most charismatic, powerful orator, and thinker of all times.

WH: I totally agree with you.

Your book, **Chicken Soup for the Soul**, was number three on USA Today's best selling books for a recent five year period. That's quite an accomplishment.

MVH: We're astounded because there are great writers out there. But what we are, is compilers of stories. We think everybody has a story to tell.

For example, the other day I was in Nashville. I'm walking out of the station and a lady grabs my arm and says, "Dr. Hansen, can I tell you a story?" I said, "Have at it." She said that she was in church yesterday here in Nashville, and the minister said, "There are two little boys, one five and one seven. They've loaded up their guns and were going to go hunting and then on to breakfast. The five year old is flaying the gun around. big brother says, 'Don't do that you idiot, that thing's loaded.' He aimed the gun at him, pulled the trigger, and blew a bullet straight through his head."

Grandpa's outside, runs in, sees the commotion and the mess, grabs the kid up, rushes him off to the hospital. This little five year old gets on his hands and knees and says, "God, God, God, you let my big brother live and heal him somehow. I don't know how you're going to do it, but if you do, I'll be the best preacher man in the whole world."

Big brother gets to the hospital and the doctor says, "I'm sorry sir, but we don't do trauma care here. We're going to have to jump in an ambulance and go to a trauma center." On the way there he says, "Look, this kid has lost so much of his brain with that bullet, that he'll never be ambulatory....never walk again." All the stuff that you know. The subconscious never sleeps..... so the big brother is hearing all this and says, "God, you let me live and I don't know what will happen, but somehow I'm going to be the best surgeon in the whole wide world."

Then the minister says, "As you can see ladies and gentlemen, I have a congregation of over 5000 and I did what I said I'd do. But I've got to tell you, my big brother is the number one pediatric neurosurgeon and teacher over at Vanderbilt University, so I think he did what he said he'd do too."

WH: That's wonderful.

MVH: Isn't that good?   Doesn't that give you goose bumps? Don't you think everybody has a life assignment?   I mean, you must believe that, or you wouldn't call your show **Share Your Mission.**

WH: I certainly do, and I think that the reason people get into such problems with addictions, is that they get distracted by outside influences. They got off track. They don't have their vision focused on their life's mission. If they did, they wouldn't be pulled away by alcohol, drugs, people, relationships, food, negative thinking, and all the rest.

MVH: Right. What they are trying to do is to anesthetize themselves.

WH: Yes. They find an emptiness in their life and they can't put their finger on the cause for it. The emptiness they feel is that they don't know what their mission is and they're not pursuing it.

MVH: Let me talk to that for a second. As we're ready to flip centuries here and millenniums as it were. We're asking everybody to write 101 goals. What we're trying to do is get ten million Americans, before the end of this year, to write 101 goals and ask them to pretend they're twelve years old, because at twelve you don't have any resistance. You knew you weren't writing the ten commandments, so they weren't marble, so you're willing to do them. I say, pretend you've got a body mask in front of you and view it with wisdom and then just wrap it over your head. So you're writing these 101 goals out of wisdom. Then I want everyone to send me a copy, not the original, and I'll send it back to them in a year. Wouldn't you like to see a year from now, when your goals come back and say, "Holy cow, I had no idea I could do that much."

WH: Yes, that would be great. What e-mail address should they send that to?

MVH: Send it to <u>laura@markvictorhansen.com</u>   What we're trying to do is just get that done, and then I'm trying, I'm not trying, I'm *going* to do a book called, **Goal Master: 101 People's Goals**, because I say you can never look at anyone else's 101 goals, without it changing your life.

I always wanted to read the Bible, but I never wrote it down as a goal, so I never put a time frame on it and never did it. Today there's such good things as a one minute Bible, so you can just whip through it one story per day. They've gotten it down to just one page a day . If everyone would set goals, we'd change the world. If you have a renewed mind, a renewed soul, a renewed hope, a renewed vision, and you need to write down both tangible and intangible, big and little, do it.

For 31 years I was single. I had written down that my ideal wife would be an intellectual voluptuary with self discipline tendencies to hedonism. That's a joke of course. But I out married myself. We get remarried every year on our anniversary in front of a minister. It really works and we have a big party. Two years ago we hired the Shirrells to come out and sing *We're Coming to the Chapel, I'm Going to be Married.* Now in a couple of days, we're getting married for the 20th time.

It's nice to have a mission and have missions within your mission, don't you think?

WH: Yes absolutely!. That's what having a happy, successful life is all about.

You talk about overcoming life's challenges and obstacles in *Chicken Soup For The Unsinkable Soul.* It's a wonderful book. Do you have anything that you can share in your personal life about obstacles and challenges that you've overcome?

MVH: Oh boy, do I. In graduate school, I knew one of the brightest guys on the planet, a guy named Dr. Buckminster Fuller. He had 2,000 major patents including the geodesic dome. I think he was Albert Einstein's best student. What happened was, I was building two million dollars worth of domes a year by the time I was 26 in New York. And I thought I was really somebody. Luckily, fortunately, I went bankrupt. It was my best-worst experience. I was upside down. The oil embargo hit and I was building a plastic product at the time: PVC. One day I was rich, the next day I'm a have-not, totally upside down. And it's at that time I discovered who I really was supposed to be, because I listened to a tape by the dean of speakers, Cavert Robert. It was called: *Are You The Cause or Are You The Effect?* It said either you are a creature of circumstance or the creator. And I thought, holy cow, if I created this bankruptcy, I had created and recreated, then I said what do I want to do? I said, " I want to talk to people who care about things that matter, that will make a life-changing difference, very much in line with what your mission is.

Since then, I've gotten to talk to a lot of people. Before I was a speaker that wrote, and now I guess you've got to say I'm a writer that speaks, because we've got so many books out. But this new *Chicken Soup for the Unsinkable Soul*, is just sort of what the doctor ordered because it's on the New York Time's best seller list right now.

What happens is that most people are going through more challenges, or at least they feel like they're going through more challenges, more than ever in history. Maybe you can talk to why that is....... then I'll do a story if you don't mind. Why do you think that is Winn?

WH: It seems to me that technology is speeding up everything. It's not like it was even ten years ago.

MVH: You're a medical doctor, and your whole body is technology that changes..... by the way, correct me if I'm wrong, but someone told me once that 50 million cells a minute change. The body is a piece of technology, wouldn't you agree?

WH: Yes. A day, or a week, or a month from now, you don't have the same body that you had before. It's all turning over and it's all new. How you treat it, not only with what you put in your mouth, but how you think..... the thoughts that you have in your mind..... determines whether it's going to be healthy, whether it's going to give up and die, whether it's going to get chronic diseases processes. And I really believe that one of the significant things that will be discovered as time goes on, is that many, or most, of the chronic disease processes come from how you think about things. If you're angry, certain disease processes are going to happen to you on a more frequent basis. If you're resentful, or if you have frequent negative feelings, then you're going to have different problems. If you can rid yourself of these emotions, you'll be a much healthier person and live a longer life.

MVH: You're right. If you think angry, hostile thoughts with hatred, resentment, envy, jealousy, and all the negative stuff, that you're going to down trodden yourself and rip yourself apart. That's why I think everyone needs to read a positive story or read the Bible every day.

WH: It certainly would help people, if they could, all the time, be thinking on the bright side, the optimistic side, the enthusiastic side, as opposed to the negative side, which is what you see in our society most of the time these days.

Let's tell them a story. I want to read a short one.

Benny's Balloon

Benny was 70 when he died rather suddenly of cancer in Wilmott, Illinois. Because his 10-year-old granddaughter Rachel, never got a chance to say goodbye, she cried for days. But after receiving a big red balloon at a birthday party, she came home with an idea: a letter to Grandpa Benny airmailed to Heaven in her balloon. Rachel's mother didn't have the heart to say no, and she watched with tears in her eyes as the fragile balloon bumped its way over the trees that lined the yard and disappeared.

Now two months later, Rachel received a letter postmarked from a town 600 miles away in Pennsylvania. "Dear Rachel, your letter to Grandpa Benny reached him. He really appreciated it. Please understand that material things can't be kept in Heaven, so they had to send the balloon back to earth. They just kept the thoughts, the memories, the love, and things like that in Heaven. Rachel, whenever you think about Grandpa Benny, he knows, and is very close by with overwhelming love for you. Sincerely, Bobby Anderson (also a grandpa.)

This is just one typical story from the book. It's really good.

MVH: I think you might remember..... do you remember Jimmy Durante? The schnooz.....Thank you Mrs. Calabash, wherever you are.

WH: Sure.

MVH: At the end of World War II, Ed Sullivan, who had a really big show, called him up and said "Look, all the boys are back from the war, and I'm entertaining them. I know you've got a TV show tonight, but I've set a limo up. You've got to come down and present for five minutes.

And after a lot of haranguing, he came down. So he goes on five minutes, then ten, then twenty and then twenty-five, and Ed comes on and says, what are you doing?

He said, "Look in the front row." And he saw one soldier who had lost his right arm. One had lost his left and together they were clapping. He said, "That's the best applause I've ever had in my life."

WH: There's just so many great stories out there if people had the opportunity to be able to hear them, and experience them..... that's what we try to do with this program. It's to bring people with different life styles, different missions..... where you can find out what they're doing, how it's affected their life. These stories just change the world.

MVH: What we want to do is..... we'd like to have everyone tell us their best story.....and we'll put it in a future book. We've got 74 more books in the queue right now. One of the books we've got coming out next year is called ***Chicken Soup For The Expectant Mother Soul.***

Are you a GP or a psychiatrist, or what do you do?

WH: I did emergency medicine and then went into family practice, and after that, addiction medicine. I'm retired now from active practice.

MVH: Well great, on all counts.

We think that women talk a little bit more than men, and we think that pregnant women always have more stories to tell than maybe anyone else, or more discovery process and how we're going to do this delivery and all that. So that's why we've done ***Expectant Mothers***. We're just finishing , so now if somebody's got great stories out there, we want to hear them.

WH: Great. We would have them send their stories to your web site?

MVH: Yes, the web site's good, or the address is in the book. There was a time when I was in college. As I told you, it was Dr. Fuller to whom someone wrote a letter:

Dr. Buckminster Fuller, % The World, and it got to him somehow...... so..... I don't think we're that famous, or probably never will be, but as I said, "Isn't that cute that somebody could write, just write "% The World" and it would still arrive at his office?"

WH: That's right. I was looking at some old postcards last night from 1901. They just wrote the person's name on there and the town. It's a lot different these days. If you don't get the exact address, including the four digit extension on the zip code, you may not get it to where you want it to go..

MVH: That's true. My parents are Danish immigrants. It's interesting. My oldest brother and I were together the other day in Florida and he said he wrote back to my aunt, who we met when we were little kids, and he got a letter back two years later. The postman wrote, "Look, I don't think anyone else is going to tell you this, but I just want you to know that your Auntie died. He wrote that on the front and addressed it himself and mailed it back to my big brother. Isn't that amazing?

WH: We're talking today with Mark Victor Hansen, the co-author of the **Chicken Soup for the Soul** series, one of the best selling book series in the world forever, I guess. He's got much more to do, and this is his mission in life.... to help people by telling stories that help them with their lives.

I think you also have some other sub-missions. You have a thing for the rain forest, don't you?

MVH: I absolutely do. I want to have everybody plant three trees. Right now, our parents out of great love and total ignorance and our forbears, destroyed many forests for houses, roads, hospitals, hotels and hama-hama-hama. So we're 18 billion trees short. There are six billion of us alive right now on this planet. so..... and I'm being an idealist here, but if everybody would plant three trees, mother nature would know we're going in the right direction. It would be nice if you planted three trees in Knoxville......you could do apple trees and then, they would bear fruit for future generations, and it would be great to eat organic, and maybe for some people that are hungry, they would get a free apple every once in a while.

WH: And we get the secondary benefit of all that oxygen.

MVH: That's really what I'm trying to do,   because earth is a little too polluted right now. We've raised one degree in heat and we're starting to melt the ice caps. It seems simplistic.   Three trees will do it.   One tree for being born........one for if you ever fell in love.......and in Israel they always plant one tree for everyone who dies........which I think is noble..... a very nice thing to do. Lose one life and gain a new kind of life.

WH: You've convinced me, I'm going to go out and buy three trees this weekend, and plant them. I hope everybody that's listening today will go out and plants three trees. If you buy some fruit trees, you'll even have the benefit of having something to eat.

MVH: Jack and I choose a different charity for each book, and one of the charities we did was to.... we're trying to reforest the planet, so last year, we personally planted a quarter billion trees with the Arbor foundation. Then we said to them, what we want to do here is to challenge the whole publishing industry. Whether you publish a DayTimer type thing, whether you publish newspapers, books, periodicals, newsletters, or anything, plant as many trees as you use up.

The fact of the matter is, until right now.... God bless the lumberjacks.   They're doing two for one but that's not enough.   It's not fast enough to suck up all that carbon dioxide, so we're saying, "Look, everybody, let's plant some trees, get rid of the carbon dioxide, and make the earth a great totally breathable, lovable place all over again. So thank you for planting three trees in advance of doing it, and thank all your listeners for doing the same.

WH: Mark, let's talk about the book for a second.   What story in this particular book stands out to you?

MVH: I think there's a couple. One that comes to mind is from Erma Bombeck. Erma Bombeck unfortunately, died of liver cancer, but she handled it with a sense of humor and a aplombness, just perfectly. She kept going to the oncologist, and they'd always tell her go down to room number four or whatever, and take off all her clothes. So she goes there and they tell her to go down to room number four and there's four guys in there dressed in suits. She's so used to the protocol that she starts taking off her clothes. And these guys mouths drop open and she says, "What's wrong?" She said, "Aren't you guys oncologists? They said, "No, we're the painting guys." But the fact that she saw it with such humor and she handled it with such savoir faire and penasch is such a nice thing, it seems to me. All of us get caught in situations that don't work for us once in a while. Hasn't that ever happened to you?

WH: It sure has.

You can look at anything as a cup half empty, or a cup half full. Everything in life can be looked at 180 degrees from the way that other people look at it. If you would turn it around and look at it the best possible way, your life would be so much happier.

MVH: Oh, by the way, there's a perfect story about that. We call it *Black and White*, and it's in **Chicken Soup for the**

Kids' Soul. These two kids are arguing. The teacher says, "Okay, Johnny you go stand at that wall. Sandy, you go stand at that wall." She pulls something out of the desk and it's a ball. She puts it in the center of the desk and says, "Sandy, what color is this?" He says, "White. "Johnny, what color is it?" Black. Black, white, black, white, and they're arguing. She says, "Okay, you guys can't reconcile this. Now, go to the other side of the room and look at it from the other perspective." And the ball was half-painted white and half-painted black.

WH: Great example. Mark, you've got how many types of ***Chicken Soup for the Soul,*** out right now?

MVH: There are 26. We've got one out that I think you'll be particularly fond of, called ***Chicken Soup for the Christian Soul.*** There's a great story in there called, *There Are No Coincidences.* It's a cold winter night this time of year and there's been an early frost. There's black ice on the highways, the tree branches are broken, and it's late at night. The Catholic priest, Father O'Malley, gets a call at 1:30 in the morning. He's just finished working on his sermon for the next day and it sort of shakes him out of his slumber. It says, " Father, we're sorry, but we've got Tom down here who's got a failing liver and he's just about ready to die. He needs for you to come in and do the last rites. So Father O'Malley gets dressed and goes out in the bitter cold night.

The half hour drive takes two and a half hours. He gets to the hospital and the wind almost blows the door off, and it shivers his timbers. He shuffles across the black ice, because it rained and then had a quick freeze. He goes into the hospital and the nurse grabs him and says, Father O'Malley, hurry, the guy's only got a few minutes left. Father O'Malley gets in the room and says, "Tom, I was in the neighborhood and I thought I'd drop by. Tom says, "Cut the bull, you weren't in the neighborhood. I asked for the last rites, now give them and get out." He says, "Look my friend, if you ever want to confess anything or admit anything or say anything, now is the time to do it." Tom says, "Look, what I did was so awful, ugly, and terrible..... God can't forgive me and you can't forgive me either."

So Father O'Malley schmoozes with him for about an hour and at the end of which he sees the vital signs are down to the last two minutes. He says, "You've got about two minutes to go. I'm reading your signs." He says, "If you're ever going to say anything, now is the time." Tom says, "Well, nobody can do anything to me now. I guess I can tell you. He said, "It happened 24 years, two months and two hours ago. That's how heavy it is in my heart. My whole life I've been a railroad switchman, and I've been an alcoholic. This night was cold, muggy and I went out to switch the railroad track. I was drunk and I switched the wrong track. The train went right into a car and killed the mother, the ather, and the two daughters. Like I said, "You can't orgive me, and God can't forgive me."

ather O'Malley puts his hand on Tom and said, "God and I an forgive you. You see she was my mother, he my father, ny two older sisters. And that's what made me decide to ecome a priest. We all forgive you.

WH: That's a touching story.

MVH: Isn't that good? You and I know that there's only two arts to love. One is givingness and the other is orgivingness. The hard part's which one?

WH: The hardest is forgiving.

MVH: Yes. The hard part of forgiving is forgiving yourself. orgive your teachers, forgive the bad boss because you and I have gone through a lot of school with bad eachers, you can forgive the bad system, you can do all kinds of stuff. But you don't want to forgive yourself. Seventy times seven, that's 490 times you need to write out, 'I forgive me, I forgive me', and then you forgive your mom and then forgive dad. It's amazing what will happen if you do hat. It'll clear you up so you can do your mission and it gets you out of a lot of self-sabotaging behavior.

WH: That's right.

We're been talking with Mark Victor Hansen today, and it's the end of our half hour. Mark we really want to thank you for being on the show today. You've told us some great stories that are really going to help some people. Mark, thank you.

MVH: It's been a joy. Thanks for having me on. I look forward to talking to you again, Dr. Winn.

Brian Klemmer

WH: Our guest today is Brian Klemmer. Brian has been professionally speaking and doing workshops for over twenty years all around the world, whether it be Japan, Spain, or the Philippines. He has been to Norway, Sweden, and Canada and has extensively traveled all over the United States.

Brian owns a leadership development company called Klemmer & Associates, which is on the West Coast. He has clients which include well-known companies such as Hewlett Packard, Walt Disney, Los Angeles Credit Union, Suzuki Motor Company, several small manufacturer businesses, financial institutions, hospitals, and sales organizations. He is a West Point graduate with a Master's Degree and a member of the National Speakers Association.

Brian's firm specializes in large bottom-line changes in a short period of time through shifting the values and fundamental beliefs of the individuals within the company organization. The unique experience and interactive nature of these workshops and seminars produce immediate and long-term results. Brian is published in a number of trade magazines and he has a new book called, *If How-To's Were Enough, We Would All Be Skinny, Rich and Happy.*

Brian is a regular keynote speaker at conventions with several thousands of people in the network marketing industry and conducts leadership and growth development training in over half a dozen network marketing companies.
How are you doing, Brian?

BK: I am doing great! Thank you very much for letting me be a part of the program, I really appreciate it!

WH: You have an interesting biography and I am going to give you an opportunity right at the beginning here to add anything that I might have missed or if you want to add anything from the day you were born until now. How did you get to where you are now?

BK: I had a mentor named Tom who was the most major influence in my life. I wouldn't be in the business I am in, I wouldn't be a Christian, I wouldn't be married if it wasn't for him. I think the mentor- ship process is a key to someone growing fast. Once you find somebody that is a kind person, has positive qualities, and walks the talk.....in other words, they are not just an outside shell, but they practice what they preach and in essence, they surrender to that. Obviously, that has Christian implications, and just like any religion is the way to grow.

WH: I totally agree with you. Having a mentor is so important. This person, Tom, did he teach you about the business you are in right now?

BK: Absolutely! I attended a seminar with him back in 1975. I was in the Army and a graduate of West Point. I ended up resigning my commission and going to work for him. I bought into a dream.

Our mission statement is "A world that works for everybody with no one left out." That is really what my company is all about! Whether it's an individual, a company, or a country, it's creating an environment where everybody has a life which is fulfilling and enjoyable.

WH: One of the greatest mentors of all time and one of my mentors was Jesus. We can't personally talk to him like you could with Tom, but in the Bible we have plenty of opportunity to learn wisdom from what he taught while he was on this earth. The amount of things that you can get from your mentor is unbelievable!

Without a direction for your life, without someone to emulate, you take so much more time and effort to achieve your goals. You keep doing things wrong. So, a mentor is a great thing to have!

Tell me about your company and what it does.

BK: We operate off the premise that 99% of all the decisions a person makes, they don't make because their belief system is made for them! That is a startling statistic and we don't have people who believe it, we just operate on that and ask people to explore that possibility.   They have belief systems about responsibility, commitment, who they think they are and how they think life works. That makes decisions for them in how they talk and interact with people, how they try to manage and sell, and how they try to be intimate with a spouse or child. They think they are choosing, but they are not!

Once the belief system changes, you don't have to motivate a person. The analogy I like to use is, "If a person was wearing a dark pair of sunglasses for their whole life and they are looking at a piece of paper on their desk and it is green because of the glasses, I would argue with you and tell you that you are wrong because I see it as white. When the person realizes they are wearing sunglasses and pulls them off, they discover what they could not see seconds before just like a revelation. It reveals something to that person which was there before but they could not see it.

We work with companies and individuals. They want results, or they want a better profit line, better sales, a better, more intimate relationship with their spouse or children, but they can't see it happening. What we have them do, in an experimental way through exercises and games, is to explore what type of sunglasses they are wearing which is preventing them from getting what they really want!

WH: So, there are some specific types of things you teach, that show people how to explore the possibility that their belief system could be wrong.

BK: Yes, but not so much wrong as not working for that particular scenario. In other words, you can develop a belief systems that works in one environment such as on your job where you have a wall up and you are not used to communicating your feelings. You can't survive in certain situations if your feelings are out there. So, your mind goes, "Oh, that's how the world is...the way you survive is not to share your feelings!" You then go to another environment such as your wife and kids, and you are operating off the same belief system but it is not working in that territory. What happens is we grow up! A lot of people believe that they have a belief system different from other people, because that's what it looks like. Their eyes tell them it looks like they are on the East Coast and others are on the West Coast. That tells them that they are separate from other people and they will operate out of separateness. No matter how many win-win team books they read, their decisions will be made accordingly. That is the kind of thing we have people explore.

WH: Basically, would a person have to be dis-satisfied with some part of their life before they would even start to explore the possibility of the type of work that you do?

BK: Dissatisfaction or a glimpse of what is possible more than they have.....there is a whole set of sunglasses we could go into. Many people have happiness tied to results. That is what they are chasing.....something with which to be happy versus knowing that happiness is a state of being you bring with you and that you can be happy no matter where you are!

Most people in their heart of hearts believe happiness is tied to results. From that perspective, they would need to be dissatisfied or have a glimpse of what is possible that is much bigger than what they say!

I have a story about dogs and bones. I ask people if dogs like bones and most people will say yes. I say, "no they don't!" People will not believe this, and I will say to them, "They like steaks, but they just settle for bones!" They get fed bones so much that they are convinced they just like bones. It is not that they dislike bones, but they are fed them so much they get used to them! If they were to set the table, they would get the steak and we would get the bones!

I think that, especially in America, we have had it so good for so long for so many people, and even if we haven't, whatever stage of life we are at it is very easy to fall into settling for what we have rather than going for what is possible.

WH: You talked about happiness and belief systems. My belief is that most people in this country believe that happiness comes from a bigger bank account, a fancier car, a better family, etc, but I believe that happiness is an internal situation that, over the long term comes from realizing what's your destiny, your mission in life, and then pursuing it and having success in fulfilling that mission!

What are your thoughts on that situation?

BK: I think that is a great way of saying it. Many people are wired in their heads the way they think at a subconscious level. They have collapsed fact and meaning and will take something such as money and make it mean something like security. I know people who have worked thirty years to accumulate money in order to be secure and yet they are very insecure and are afraid of losing it. They start seeing that the meaning side of things does not reside in the factual side of things. I believe it is the same with happiness. It does not reside in the same place in which all the things which you mentioned reside. It is in a whole different realm!

When I first got married sixteen years ago, I was three months behind on the mortgage of my house. I was in question as to whether I was going to continue in my job. My whole life was in an upheaval and yet, I was very happy!

My wife bought me a $19 K-Mart wedding ring because she had no money either. She was a single mom with two kids when I married her, yet we were very happy! Now, our financial situation is way different! God has blessed us very well, and we are still happy!

People still put attachments to things. They think you can't have money and be spiritual or you can't have money and be happy! I think like you that they have confused what realms or domains things exist in.

I just love the work you do with self-esteem. So many people out there are trying to increase their self-esteem from what I call an outside approach. It is a very short-lived thing. It is similar to behavior modification because you can change a person's behavior for short-term, such as people trying to lose weight, most times, their internal systems are going to dictate they way they are. If they change from the inside out, which is what I believe that they should do, they will change for the better.

WH: That is exactly right! If you don't believe something with every cell inside of your body, it doesn't really make any difference what your mouth says, because it is not going to come through in terms of results! No matter how many times people pat you on the head and tell you that you are a good person.... if you don't believe that on the inside, it is not going to do you any good!

BK: I was just with Shawna Gerber who attended one of our seminars. She, a Canadian, and her husband Nick, were on their way to divorce and living in separate households when one of them attended our seminar a year ago. After the seminar, they are back in the same household, happily married. Their financial situation is five times better, and they own their own home now. Many people would look at them and say it's a miracle. In one sense it was, but all it was, was a dramatic change in a short period of time because some belief systems, some sets of sunglasses, came off and they were able to pierce that veil and see things differently. Once they saw it differently, they began to rebuild.

Unlike a how-to, and that is the title of my book, *If How-To's Were Enough, We Would All Be Skinny, Rich and Happy.* So many people are trying to improve their life from a how-to versus having a revelation and changing the set of sunglasses. This takes a fraction of a second versus how-to which takes practice and practice and practice. It is a long endeavor.

WH: We are talking today with Brian Klemmer who is the head of Brian Klemmer & Associates. You can go to their web site at www.klemmer.com and see the neat things they are doing. If you want to give them a call, their number is 415-898-0848 or you can call

1-800-577-5447 which is also a way to get a copy of Brian's new book. It's also available on amazon.com.

Brian, please summarize your book for the listeners.

BK: The book is very much based on the talk about sunglasses that I have been doing today. It has some fundamental beliefs that people will deal with in their lives.

One has to do with results around commitment, one has to do with responsibilities. For example, most people think responsibility is a burden or a duty or an obligation. When a parent tells a child or a boss tells an employee they must be more responsible, they hear it or see it as work! They believe they are already working as hard as they can.....so nothing changes. If you can get a truck driver to see how responsibility is exciting and powerful and how they are responsible for the profit and loss of the whole company, you don't have to motivate that truck driver, they will automatically do their job differently!

I have people in the book explore responsibility, commitment.....their own vision, which you deal with .....the whole notion of separateness. They explore some of the fundamental beliefs which affect their life at home and at work.

WH: Let me give you an opportunity to tell the audience something you have been waiting to say all your life.

BK: *You can have the life you want to have.* That is such a cliche but its true! The lack that exists in the world today, in all corners of the world, not just in the United States, is unnecessary! One of the primary belief systems that most people have going is one of scarcity and if they can attack that whether through me or some other way they can have hope. I guess that's the biggest thing I want to say.

I am a merchant of hope because I believe that whatever people are going through, they can get better in a short period of time as long as they are willing to look at their belief systems. If they are willing to do that, dramatic changes can happen over a short period of time.

This is what excites me about life.....to look at people and see the dramatic changes that have happened. It doesn't matter if it is a CEO of a company or an individual on the streets who has almost no hope. That excites me because I like making a difference.

WH: You talked about lack and scarcity. One belief system is that there is not enough to go around and there must be some kind of competition.....either I get it and you lose, or vice versa. Therefore I have to fight somebody else to get what I need, but that is not right is it? Each of us in our lives have the ability if we knew that we were not limited to do whatever we want to do, and it is not taking away from somebody else to get what we need!

BK: That is very accurate and deeply seeded. This whole idea of separateness is what causes the competition. If we imagine two islands and all we look at is above the water, the two islands appear separate. One might appear beautiful and one might be desolate. One might be populated and the other unpopulated, but beneath the water they are connected.
Most people are operating only above the water line so they see themselves as different such as one is talkative and one is shy, or one is black and one is white. Out of that comes the competition, and that is one of the main things that we address because it affects every area of our life.

Let's talk about statistics.....one in seven people have health insurance today, one in eight drop out of school. If school was a business, we would be out of business! It is not working, but it can work! One in four individuals had a mother who did not graduate from high school. To me that is unbelievable. One in one hundred and twenty die before their first birthday in this country! This is one of the most medically advanced country in the world, yet that kind of infant mortality is totally unnecessary! If you look at the rest of the world, it is the same thing. A portion of the world does not have safe sanitation or water. 20% of the world doesn't have proper shelter and 33% goes to bed hungry every night! I am not saying that is doom and gloom, but I am saying that I am glad we have the technology today to work with people so they can see that is not the way it has to be! It all starts at an individual level.

You need to have the outlook that you are in total alignment with each other. A person can look around and see no way their situation can improve, but if I can communicate to them that there is hope, then they can realize that it only takes a minimal amount of effort to take off those sunglasses and see the world differently.

WH: Thank you so much for being with us today, Brian.

BK: Thank you, Winn. I hope I have contributed something useful to your listeners.

Don Blue

VH: Today we have the pleasure of having Donald Blue with us from San Antonio, Texas. Don has a rich career history in health care administration, customer service, time management, and sales training. He is also a former educator and served in the Special Forces. We are going to talk with him today. Don, how are you doing?

DB: I am fantastic!

VH: Let's go back and talk about your life. You were born in the South and then moved to the North. Tell us what happened.

DB: I didn't have a whole lot of choice in that move. My parents wanted to move from Alabama to the steel mill town of Pittsburgh because it offered greater job opportunities for my father. So I grew up in the north.

VH: You didn't have it really well in your early years did you? You didn't come with a silver spoon in your mouth!

DB: No. Unfortunately, my father died when I was twelve and my mother was of poor health. So as a result, I had to work through junior high school and high school to afford not only extra things like going to the show but also to help my mother put food on the table, buy clothes, and pay the house rent.

WH: I have been in the business of helping people with various types of addictive problems for the last 20 years. You have some experience with alcohol problems in your family don't you?

DB: My father had been a drinker for a great portion of his life, which probably led him to having a fatal heart attack at the age of 52 . He had stopped drinking for about 2 years before he died, but unfortunately, it wasn't soon enough. There wasn't enough time to really build a relationship with him.

WH: So, you have some personal experience with those type of problems?

DB: Yes I do!

WH: You then went into high school and became an athlete. Tell us about that.

DB: I have had many blessings. Being an athlete was probably my first. I ran track, played baseball, and football. As a result of my ability to run and carry a football, I was able to mingle and have friends who did not live in my neighborhood........in public housing. I was able to see how other people lived. I saw how people who were successful lived. I realized that there wasn't a great amount of difference between them and myself except where they slept at night. By seeing this, it gave me belief that higher goals were something to strive for and that they were achievable. My relationships with these individuals became my source of strength.

WH: You played football at Kansas University, didn't you?

DB: Yes I did.

WH: After that experience you went on and joined the Army, right?

DB: Yes. That was very enriching for me. I went in the Army not knowing exactly what I wanted to be as a young man. I was afforded the opportunity to go into the special forces. The required training em-powered me tremendously. It gave me leadership skills. It showed me that I had courage to do things I never thought I would be able to do. I was also able to learn several different languages and travel to many different foreign countries.

WH: You were with the Green Beret's.

DB: Yes, I was.

WH: As I understand, you received many medals when you were in Vietnam.

DB: That's correct. Medals were given for many reasons, most reasons centered on being involved in actual combat in the field. I was in an action unit during my four years in Vietnam. Since I went to the field very frequently, I received several medals.

WH: After that experience, you started working with *Young Adult Ministry*, correct?

DB: Yes. While we lived in Chicago, I was part of a program called *Theology on Tap*. It was a springtime series of programs where we went out into the community and spoke with young adults who had either been away from the church or had never gone to church. It was truly enriching. Father Cusik in Chicago has a tremendous ministry there.

WH: About how long did you do that kind of work, Don?

DB: I had been active with this program at Old Saint Patrick's church in Chicago for about four years before we moved to San Antonio. Now every time we go up there for business, I make it a point to go back to Old St. Pat's because it is our spiritual home.

WH: After that, what was the next thing in your life?

DB: I became a grandfather. We moved back to San Antonio to be close to our first grandson. And to be flexible with my time, build on my experiences, and help others to achieve greater success, I started *Leadership Concepts*. My focus is to provide workshops on various aspects of leadership. My goal during a workshop is to empower individuals to grow and create positive experiences, regardless of the circumstances that are presented to them. Most people limit themselves to being successful only "when the circumstances are right." The problem with that is that rarely in our personal life or our work endeavors are the circumstances just right! Basically, I want them to see how they can be successful through their own actions.

Other people limit themselves by believing that they have to be intelligent in order to succeed. That is just not true. There are many people who are highly educated who are unemployed or can't maintain a job or a relationship. My workshops give them tools that they can use to help them create and realize their dreams and goals.

WH: You are working on a new book that is going to be published this year.

DB: It is a book for supervisors, especially new supervisors. It will give them a road map to follow to help them be successful as supervisors.

WH: Do you have a title for it yet?

DB: Yes! It's very simple: **Supervision 101**.

WH: That sounds like a book you might pick up at your local college!

DB: That is exactly where we are going first.

WH: It is important, I believe, in life to learn from the experiences of others and I have had mentors in my life. I wonder if you have ever had a mentor or teacher in your life that has taught you something that is valuable that you might share with us.

DB: This is another area where I have been blessed. Through various stages in my life, I have had four mentors.

I met my first mentor in high school, Mrs. Stone. She encouraged me to go for more, even though I lived in public housing. She was sure to remind me that if I kept reaching for the stars that I would get it.

When I was in working on my Master's Degree in Education, Dr. Knight was my mentor. She was terrific. She not only encouraged me, but she also showed me that having grown up without a father was a valuable lesson to share with young children. Because, as you know, in today's society there are many households where there is no father, no role model or man that they can talk to. I had not realized I could learn so much from that event. My emotions would not step aside long enough to learn. Dr. Knight was able to help me to focus on what it was like and how to grow up without having developed that relationship.

WH: What do you think is the most important thing a person could do, with respect to mentoring their children? What advice would you give parents with respect to teaching them?

DB: I think one of the key things I have noticed about my children and my friends' children is that children will mimic what their parents do, even to the point that they will walk around the house with a crayola in their mouths pretending to smoke because their parents smoke. In other words, you should do very positive things in front of your children. They will pick up everything you do and say so be focused on being the way you want them to be.

WH: I am curious as to what you think of success because

you are a motivational speaker and you give seminars and lectures on motivational topics. What is success to you? How do you define it?

DB: I see myself as an entrepreneur, a risk taker, great as a bull, aggressive, willing to attempt new ideas and seek new paths. A lot of people ask me "Why do you do this?" My potential to achieve is backed by the power of Christ.

Philippines 4:13 says "I can do all things through Christ who strengthens me."

WH: What is success to you? It's not money necessarily. How would you define it in terms of your own personal values?

DB: To give, not necessarily money, but give time. Give encouragement. A lot of people think "I can't afford to give!" I see giving as sowing a seed. You are going to reap something from it. It may not be money that you receive, but you will receive something by giving, even if you are poor.

WH: That's right! Even if we don't have money at this particular time, we always have time that we can give. Giving of yourself sometimes seems much more valuable to me than writing a check.

There are four important spiritual questions in life that I talk about in my book and whenever I get a chance to speak. The third question is: *What am I doing here?* In other words, what is my destiny, my mission in life? It's important because over the last 20 years, I have found in addiction counseling that people who don't have a purpose, don't have a mission, and are not focused on something...... or don't have a priority, are easily drawn away by things in the external environment that tend to pull them and also harm them. Most of these addictive behaviors will cause some kind of pain or suffering, and it generally doesn't take very long to experience it.

However.......if a person has a mission......has something they are focused on, they tend not to be pulled away by these externals.
I'm wondering, Don, what is your mission in life?

DB: My mission in life involves giving not only money but also my time. More specifically, I want each and every person I meet throughout the world, to look at each other not by the color of their skin but as human beings. I want to help them get past physical barriers. To do this I help them understand relationships.

WH: Do you get the feeling that by having a service mission like that and by focusing on that, that it makes it easier for you to resists these things in the world that would tend to pull you away from your mission?

DB: Absolutely. Keeping focused on my mission energizes me, especially when I am giving a speech on leadership or motivation, and I look into the audience and see the faces light up and heads nodding. These responses tell me that I am reaching people and it gives me pride and hope in knowing that if I can reach one person, that person can reach out to another person. The impact of what I do will then just multiply from there.

WH: In your speeches that you have given and the things that you have shared with people, can you think of any example that you can tell us about on how this has impacted somebody's life in a positive way?

DB: The biggest reward I have had, has come from the teenagers that I was able to touch during their high school days. The school I taught in.......in Chicago was a really interesting school. Among the students, there were fourteen different languages spoken. We had kids from China, South America.....all over. One of my classes was to teach physics and science as a second language to these kids. We built relationships that continue today. They call me. They e-mail me to let me know what they are doing, how they are reaching out, how they are empowering others, and they thank me. Some of them have even said, "The days you would talk to us in school, we really didn't hear or understand the message." But now that they are out of school and they are in their professions they see it. That just makes my day.

In fact, a week ago my wife and I were in Chicago walking down Michigan Avenue and a young lady who I have not seen in seven years came up and put her arms around me. I was taken aback. She wanted to thank me for all the things that I did, and I was trying to remember what I had done.

She said, "Do you remember me? I was the bad girl in the back of the class, the one who gave you all the trouble. You didn't give up on me. You just kept giving me hope and strength. As a result of that, I graduated from college, and I now have a successful career. That just pumps me up to reach out and touch more people.

WH: That is a good example of the power of unconditional love. If you don't try to judge another person or try to manipulate them based on their behavior, but just continue to feel unconditional love for the person as a child of God, it really does a lot of good in the world. You never can tell just what it is going to do for an individual or what that individual is going to do as a result of that. That's just wonderful!

You have been a teacher in the past and you have a lot of experiences with all types of children. In your experience, what do you think might be the cause of the confusion in the way they think about values and things in life. Our society is really getting bad in the respect that children are killing other children.....adults......their parents. They are doing all kinds of things. What's the breakdown here?

DB: One of the ways I look at today's situation is that I compare how I grew up with how my own children have grown up. Even though we did not have a lot of money when I grew up and we lived in public housing, there was a sense of community. If Ms. Sarah from down the street saw me doing something wrong, she would say, "Donald!" I would straighten up just as if she were my mother. Today, people live next door to each other for years and never know each other's names or the number of kids in the community. There is no involvement. There is a phrase that says, "It takes a village to raise a family!" I think we need that, especially now when most households are supported by either single parents or two individuals working just to meet the needs of raising a family. I think it takes a village to raise kids.

WH: I think you are right on that. I was talking with Larry King three weeks ago and he said that when he was brought up in Brooklyn, they had that same sense of community there. The biggest value that they prized over all was loyalty within that community! We have a lot of trouble with commitment and loyalty these days......not only in community but also relationships and families. That is a value that we should be looking at more.

We have a country that could really use some leadership. There are some problems in this area, especially in the political arena. Give us your thoughts on leadership.

DB: I think if you look at the United States today, we are still a great country, but one in two people have lived in a single parent family at some point in their childhood. One in three 5-17 year old's are behind a grade in school. One in four are born to mothers who did not graduate from high school. One in eight drop out of school. One in twenty-five report abuse and neglect each year. What I see is that not only do we need governmental leadership and spiritual leadership, we also need community leadership to take to our children.....they are our future.

I met up with a friend in San Francisco recently and he turned on a light for me. He said, "What is your mission?" We discussed it for awhile. People think of one to twenty years out in order to accomplish their mission. He made me sit up, because he looks at his goals one hundred years out!

When I am gone and you are gone, Dr. Henderson, what did we leave behind? What I want to leave behind is to empower individuals to use their leadership skills, so that each succeeding generation will be stronger and more understanding.

WH: That is definitely a worthwhile goal, Don. One of the most important things I know of that makes a good family unit survive is good communication. I know that you talk about communication in your speeches and your seminars. Tell us some of your thoughts about communication.

DB: The most important factor in a relationship is the effective communication. By definition, communication means that a message was sent, understood, and acted upon. There are times when a message is sent that the receipt of that message is a lot different than was intended. What I try to teach is not only that an individual needs to be an effective sender, but also be an effective receiver.

WH: Praising other individuals really does a lot for their self esteem but so often we find it is hard to do for some reason or another. Either we do not think about it or it is difficult to approach that subject with people. How do you feel about praising other individuals?

DB: A leader, father, or a parent must be able to influence and inspire people. Role modeling is essentially a non-verbal process, but it may not be picked up on by many individuals. The best way to directly inspire people is to praise their good work! Praise your children for good work in school. Praise your employees or peers that they did a good job. Surveys have shown that praise and recognition are stronger motivators for employees than a bonus check.

I remember as a child, that my father used to call me "Manny." He would pat me on the head and say, "That was really good, Manny!" That was the biggest thing that he could have done for me. He could buy me ice cream, but it didn't make me feel better than that!

I tell parents to find ways to compliment their children and employers to find a way to compliment their team. It is important that when they do good things they are recognized and appreciated.

WH: That's some excellent advice.

We have been talking today with Don Blue from San Antonio, Texas. Don does public speaking and seminars of the motivational type and he has a book that is going to be coming out this year called *Supervisor 101* which is in the management line of business.

I am happy to have the opportunity to spend some time with Don today and get his ideas on a number of topics. It has been very enlightening.

I really appreciate you being on the program with us. Thank you, Don!

DB: Thank you, Dr. Henderson!

Roberta Wilkins

WH: Our guest today is Dr. Roberta Wilkins. She is a talk show host and she does other things that you will find very interesting, which we will talk about today.   Dr. Wilkins specializes in Power Therapies for the 21st Century and that is the name of her new talk show which you can hear on KFNX 1100-AM in Phoenix, Arizona and WALE 990-AM in Providence, Rhode Island.   It airs Fridays on the West coast 10 -11 a.m. PST and on the East coast 1-2 p.m. EST.

Dr. Wilkins has a degree in Naturopathy and some other degrees.   She does a new type of alternative medicine techniques to get people up and running. We are going to be talking about that also today. Her experiences in life, up to this point, have included 25 years of teaching and motivating people to be their best under whatever circumstances they find themselves.   She has worked with corporations and individuals over this period of time, leading them to success.

Roberta was born in Germany and grew up in an orphanage until the age of three.   During this period of time, she suffered a number of things, including malnutrition and frostbite.   She   survived a near-fatal automobile accident during her early years.   She has had a near-death experience which we hope she will share with us today.   She has rehabilitated herself from severe injuries, including paralysis. She truly has a rich heritage and background in her own personal experiences from which to help other people change their lives.

She has 25 years experience in removing fears, phobias, and emotional and physical trauma, PTSD, and self-sabotaging behavior. She also has experience in grief, loss, performance anxiety, test anxiety, sports injuries and chronic pain. Dr. Wilkins has experience working with professional and amateurs in the corporate environment, using all she has learned during her lifetime.

She is going to be writing two books this year, one of which is named, ***Metaphors of Life***. The other will be called, ***The Voice of a Mother's Love***. We are happy to have Dr. Wilkins with us today. She is from Colorado. Dr. Wilkins, how are you doing today?

RW: I am fine. Thank you very much, Dr. Henderson.

WH: Was that bio. too long for you?

RW: No that was just great!

WH: I don't get to interview radio talk show hosts too often, except the week before last when I interviewed Larry King. He was fun to listen to. Now I have my second talk show host. Tell us anything that will bring us up-to-date to know you a little bit better and about what you are doing with your life.

RW: I truly believe that we have three minds. We have a superconscious mind, a conscious mind, and a subconscious mind. I believe that what has happened today is that people have let the subconscious mind rule them. As a result, we have lost divinity and self-worth because of early programming in life. I believe that it doesn't matter what environment we arrive in, we can change it to a positive and we can learn to love, accept, and have self-worth.

What I try to do is motivate people to realize that everybody is important and everybody is worth loving. What they need to do is to find the divinity inside of themselves and to be able to express their natural true self. We all come in this environment wanting to love and to produce. From the time we are in the womb, from birth up to around age 7-8, all the programming comes from external factors such as our parents, our grandparents, our teachers. At that time, a child cannot reason.......everything is taken into the subconscious mind which takes everything and records it. It is like a huge file system or a big computer. Everything goes in. The child only reacts to the stimulus that he or she is around. What happens then is that as we get older we allow whatever happened to us in our younger life to be able to create what is happening in our older life, which doesn't serve us anymore.

What I try to teach people to do is to bring that conscious mind that we have now and bring it together with the superconscious mind. When we bring the two together, we learn that we do not have to carry on in the same ways we handled things when we were younger.

An example of this is......I have athletes to come in and they know how to shoot a basketball, make a free-throw, but all of a sudden they get in a panic and their statistics go down.

What happens is they have triggered something in the subconscious of their mind that tells them they are not able to succeed. Therefore, we have to go back and find what that is and bring the adult self in and push that mind up to where the person is in the present. I believe that if we live by three rules, then we find that our lives are much easier. One is to stay in the present moment. Two is to not take anything personal. When we take things personally, it is usually coming back from our past, where someone hurt our feelings. There are no judgements on anybody. Everybody is trying to do the best that they can at the time. All of our experiences here on earth are experiences in life, in how to do things, lessons that we have here on earth. I think that we are all in lessons and we learn how to deal with things. This is one giant school on earth.

My mission is to let people know that they have just as much right to be successful, to be lovable as anybody else! Also, to bring that divinity that is inside of them out so they realize that yes, they can be a loving person and produce and do things.

WH: The concept of the supraconscious, the sub-conscious, and the conscious is something that I am highly interested in. Tell me, do you remember back where you first heard of these and when you developed them in your mind?

RW: I learned about them through my school work in psychology and my training.

During my training, I was exposed to dealing with issues of

my past. As you know, when you are trained in the medical field, you have to do this, especially in the field of psychology. You need to be able to take care of your own things before you can move forward in life. That's where I have learned about how the mind works. I learned that some of the patterns I was using were not allowing me to be successful in life. By understanding these dysfunc-tional patterns, I am able to help others to go back and say, "Hey, we don't need to carry on this old habit anymore. We don't need to act this way." The inner child is acting like that, but we are the adult now, and we are in control. I learned through education, through my own life experiences, to take back the power of my life.

WH: That is really interesting because as I was coming through school, I don't remember anything specific mentioned of the concept that how the mind works being divided into the supraconscious, the conscious and the subconscious. It was only when I was doing prayer and meditation on the question of how does the mind work that I got the answer of those three ideas. I went and wrote it down.

The interesting thing in my case was that five months later I was talking to a fellow who asked me if I had ever read Edgar Casey. I said no I hadn't, and he suggested that I read Edgar Casey because he is one of the premier soothsayers of the century. I got a book by Thomas Sugrue on Edgar's life because Thomas was the only biographer to get to know Edgar personally. Casey had gone into about fourteen thousand trances and answered questions while his secretaries wrote them down. It is a tremendous story.

On page 225, or thereabout, he was in a trance and the question came up of how does the mind work and he said the same thing about the three conscious states. I thought that was a great coincidence and now, hearing it from you it is just amazing how truth permeates down through the centuries. That is a genuine concept because of the different ways it has come to us.

Carl Jung said that one's subconscious has attachments to every other individual's subconscious all over the planet. So if you are thinking one thing and your sub-consciousness is connected to someone else's sub-consciousness, even if you don't express this verbally, they are going to pick up on the vibrations of it, and it will be transmitted. Therefore, we need to watch what we actually think because those vibrations are going out into the world.

RW: Exactly! Our thoughts produce so many volts of electricity and when we speak, it is like it is half as powerful. Then, if we write it, it is three times as powerful. People don't understand how powerful their thoughts are and they are carried through a vibrational modality that people pick up and that's when we have these higher thoughts or we have these spiritual thoughts when we go into meditation. What's happening is that we are honing in on a higher vibration and we are able to pick up these types of thoughts. Our thoughts do produce how we live. We don't realize how powerful our thoughts can be!

WH: We have been talking to a number of people, in fact, I talked with Dr. Bernie Siegel yesterday on the mind/body/soul connection in medicine and it seems that more and more people are accepting the fact that diseases are caused by how you think about things.

RW: I see that in my practice. I deal with a lot of physical rehabilitation and under every ailment, there is usually an emotional or mental component. Again, we have four bodies in our system. We have a mental body, a physical body, a emotional body, and a spiritual body. If any one of these are out of balance, then what happens is that we open ourselves up to disease. We open ourselves up to injury. A lot of times when injury and disease comes to us, it is a stopping point. It is a point where we have to say, "Hey, we need to evaluate what we are doing in our lives!" It brings us to the present moment. Any disease or injury has an emotional, or mental component attached to it and that is the part that needs to be considered.....along with the traditional therapies.....to make a person whole, to balance those bodies. When you balance those bodies, you bring divinity, and you truly can lead a happy and healthy life.

WH: I agree with you! I have been working with people who have psoriasis for a number of years and I have a new treatment that is highly effective with respect to getting rid of the plaques, but getting back to the basic disease process of what causes psoriasis, I read some literature that said people with psoriasis have higher anger levels than other people and I was really interested when Dr. Siegel said that anger causes more disease than any other single entity.

RW: Anger is held so tight in the body and it is at a

vibrational level that it is to the point of the body can't handle it. What happens is that at the high vibrational levels, anger causes the body to say, "Hey, I've got a weak stomach, bingo, I am going to give you an ulcer!" Anger is a toxin in our society. I think it is one of the things that is really bringing society down. If we can learn to control our anger and move it more into a positive, then we can be more successful in our society.

Anger leads to depression. Usually, when you have people that come in and are depressed, they don't even remember how angry they were or in rage before the depression hit. The anger was the onset of all the depression. What happens when people come into my office is that we deal with depression and then we get back to the original idea of why they were so angry, what they were so enraged about. That is the healing that needs to take place so that person can move on and lead a happier life.

WH: We tend to think that most of the addictive problems that face people result from the lack of understanding certain relationships including and probably the most important one, deals with the question we explore on this program of what am I doing here? In other words, people that do not have a focus in life, don't have a purpose, don't have some destiny they want to accomplish, tend to get distracted very easily by things in the environment that make them feel good about themselves like drinking, taking drugs, controlling other people, overeating, spending too much money, and all these kinds of things. If they were to have a purpose or a mission they could focus on, they would not be pulled away or distracted as often by the externals. What do you think about that?

RW: I think that is a very valid point! We don't have focus today, and I think people do not have purpose because there's so many things going on in the environment. We look at our kids today and what's going on with the politicians and so forth. The kids say, "You're trying to teach us morals, you're trying to teach us these things? Look what is happening and the adults are getting away with this!"

It is very hard to have a focus and a purpose and I think that is probably one of the major keys that is missing today. We aren't allowed to have a focus and a purpose or we get so defeated when we try to go for it, that we don't understand. We have more defeats than successes.

Eventually, you get to your purpose providing it's a positive goal. What I mean by that is if you are not hurting anybody, not stepping on people to get where you need to go, but what you are trying to do is whatever inside propels you, whatever motivates you, whatever is your passion, is what motivates people. If you have that passion or that motivation to do whatever you are going to do, you can be successful, providing that you are not stepping on people. Now you can be successful that way but eventually it catches up with you.

WH: Are you passionate about your new radio talk show?

RW: I am very passionate about it! What I am passionate about is that it is an opportunity for me to talk to 7 million viewers. What I like about it is that I am offering things that can help them to enhance their healing whether it be mental or physical. I am able to get on the air and give hope to someone. If I can touch one or two people during that show and they can say, "Wow! I can use that modality or maybe, I am okay," then I have completed my mission.

WH: You also have a web site, I believe it is *www.x-cellperformance.com.* People can go to that site and see about all the great things that you are doing?

RW: Yes, that is true! If they go to the web site, they can get an understanding about what is going on and the different modalities that sports fitness consultants use to reach people to get at their peak performance.

WH: Tell me, how do you feel about people who want to be successful but they don't understand truly what success is?

RW: Success has to be defined by the person. I think that sometimes what happens is that the people bite off more than what they can chew and their goal is so big that they are not able to obtain it. We have to define success as what the person feels is successful. Some people feel like that if they are in a six-digit figure, they are successful in life. Other people feel like if they have touched someone's life and given them love, then they are successful. It determines what is successful to that person. Our only way that we are not successful is by our own negativity of programming that has come in and not allowed us to believe that we are just as good as anybody else.

WH: Success often means not giving up and not quitting. You will never be a failure as long as you never quit trying.....no matter how many times you are unable to reach your goal. It is when you quit that you become unsuccessful!

RW: Right! You will see that in sporting, music, or whatever. This is one thing I encourage our young people today, whether it be sports or music, they need to get into something that they really have some passion in so that they can become successful because our school system has come to the point where it kind of filters people through. I lot of kids, I don't think, have a purpose. If they had a purpose or a passion and were working towards that, they could gain so many things........through sports, through music, theater, art, or whenever there is passion........what happens is that they learn that self-discipline and they learn how it is to be successful. A lot of people do not want to take the time to be self-disciplined, to be able to practice over and over, to be able to get a skill down, they want it all just given to them. To be successful, you are right, you can not give up, you have to keep going, you have to keep working, you have to look at all different ways of getting to the goal that you deserve.

WH: I interviewed Bonnie St. John Deane a while back. She is an lady who had an amputation of her leg when she was about five-years-old and despite various things that stood in her way, she eventually received a silver medal in the World Olympics. I asked her about success and what differentiated her from other people and she said, "I just keep getting back up again every time that I fall, I just keep getting back up again! I wouldn't quit!" You're right, if you don't quit, you always have a chance at being successful.

RW: When I was in the automobile accident and was dead at the scene and brought back, I was paralyzed. I had to learn to speak all over again but one of the biggest concerns I had at this time was that I was a physical education teacher in the public schools and a high school coach and I didn't have my right hand working. I remember the physicians coming in and telling me that I would be paralyzed and that my arm would never work again. I remember in my mind that I said, "No way!" I told them I was a physical education teacher and a coach. There is no way. I have to have both my hands to be successful in my job! I never took any negativity programming that was coming in. I never accepted the fact that I was not getting my arm back! Sure, I had to work hard and I did my own rehabilitation because I was doing much more than what their rehabilitation program was doing for me. They sent me to tons of doctors that kept saying, "You are not going to get the use of your arm back," and I said, "Yes I am!" When I finally got the movement back, the physician that did most of the surgeries, my orthopedic physician, said, "I didn't do that, God and you did!" I said, "Yes, we would not accept no!"

WH: I want to ask you, you said you had a near-death experience. Will you tell me about that?

RW: I was driving to work and I was in an automobile accident. I was going 70 mph and the car that hit me head on was going 100 mph. It was in the morning and I remember being there and they were all saying that they were sending the coroner out. I was in my car, literally, up to my neck in my car and I was above the scene. I saw everything that was going on below. It was a cold morning but I was not cold at all. In fact, it was so cold that I could see the blood dripping from my head down and it was already clotting by the time it hit my chest. I was up there trying to tell people that I was fine and that I was alive, but they were convinced I was dead.

During that time, I have to admit, it was a very special time! I met some of my grandparents that had passed on, I met some friends and some people that I knew and they greeted me there. But, the biggest thing that I found out was that I was able to look at my whole life, and I looked at all the things that had happened to me and all the things that I had not done yet. You can make the decision on whether you come back or whether you go on and I made the decision because I got a message up there which whoever I met up there, it had to be God, gave me a signal that my mission was not done here and I had many more things to do and I needed to come back. I came back and that is when I began to do my work and learn how it was to help people motivate themselves. I had to do that from the start, from losing my arm, losing my speech, not being able to comprehend things, and not being able to use my mind. I had to learn all of them so that I had to understand at the ground level what people were going through. I think this is one thing that I have that when I work with people with physical ailments or they have mental problems, I understand at what ground level they are starting at because I know how hard it is to regroup, to get all of those things back! I think that was a gift for me, to get an understanding, to work with people and know what it is like to be paralyzed, to know what it is like to have to use other resources. Your other senses learn to be stronger. It's amazing. Retraining the mind. People think, "Well, you have your arm back now, how easy is that?" For years, I had to think about picking up a pencil. I couldn't pick up a pencil like we normally do. I had to think, "Okay, I need to take my thumb and my forefinger and I need to pick up the pencil and bring it over." It had to be a total mental process before the physical process could take over.

WH: Roberta, that is a terrific story about how you were able to come back from that tragic situation and we really appreciate you sharing that with us. Thank you so much for being on the program today. We have learned a lot of interesting things. I am sure that you are going to be helping a lot of people with these "power therapies for the 21st Century."

RW: Thank you, Dr. Henderson

Dr. Peter De Benedittis

WH: Good Morning!   Our Guest today is Peter De Benedittis.   Dr. DeBenidittis goes by "Dr. D". and we are going to talk to him today about something which he is very passionate about......Media Literacy.

You may be wondering what Media Literacy is.   I have the definition which I have taken off his web page: Media Literacy is the ability to read television and mass media.   It is an educational process which teaches people to access, analyze, evaluate and produce media.

Many studies suggest that such education can produce less vulnerable children and adolescents.   National PTA's, teachers organizations, substance abuse prevention programs, and the President have all endorsed Media Literacy.

Children who understand the motivations and production techniques of media are less likely to adopt a destructive attitude and behaviors that are depicted by the media.   Media education represents a new and exciting approach to protecting children and adolescents from the unhealthy effects of media...... an approach which is not part of Hollywood's or Madison Avenue's willingness to accept responsibility for its programming and advertising.

Dr. D. made the following comment I found on his web site: "I see a culture formed around humanities hearts, and desires, not manufactured by commercial greed.   I see media and entertainment that expresses,   enriches, and enhances, rather than teaches compulsive debt, substance abuse, violence, and risky behavior because there is profit in it. I see a world where everyday people have the power to shape their culture because they have access to the information and communication venues upon which democracy depends."

It is now our pleasure to welcome to our program, Dr. Peter D. How are you doing, Peter?

PD: I am doing great, thank you for inviting me!

WH: Is there anything else you would like to tell the people before we get started about you, your background, or any other tidbits?

PD: I ran an advertising agency for ten years so I kind of know how the business works. Most of my clients were political candidates so I understand polling and how production is designed to put on a certain spin on messages. These days, I sleep better at night because I teach people how they are being manipulated rather than just trying to manipulate them.

WH: You were talking about politics, do you have any insight or anything you would like to tell us while we are in the middle of this political ballyhoo? [The 2000 Presidential election]

PD: It is kind of interesting to me how the spin on both sides is taking place. It just really blows my mind. The laws they are following are written very clearly but no one is bothering to look at the laws. The whole spin is a good portrait on how our government really works. It is not about what the laws are, its about the personalities and how they spin it.

WH: It has certainly been going on for an extremely long time. I think everybody is tired of fooling with it now so maybe within a few days they will get the presidential election resolved and we can move forward.

Let's talk about your passion. It is a passion isn't it?

PD: Yes! I do this because I love doing it, and I am really in this for the long haul. I really want to see a cultural revolution take place.

WH: The thing that you do......media Literacy..... let's tell the audience.....you have presented it to more than 100,000 students in the United States over the last few years. What do you normally do? Go into a high school and make a presentation?

PD: Schools are probably my number one venue I talk to. I also work a lot with health professionals, state health departments, and teachers. I train them in how to relate this message. 85% of all media in our country.....books, magazines, television, radio and newspapers are all owned by eight corporations. If the mergers of the FCC go through, we are going to be down to about six corporations that control our media systems. That means that these six corporations have free speech and the rest of us pay for it!

After world war II, we set up provisional governments in

Germany and Japan. The members of those countries were fascists. We had to teach them how to be democratic. Both those countries said they wanted to have a centralized media system, but we said they couldn't do that because it was against democratic principles. Now, all of a sudden, fifty years later, we have lost a war. We have six or eight corporations who decide our cultural being. They also decide our political being. The presidential election we are now looking at, shows Ralph Nadar as the only legitimate candidate, and he was arrested for trying to sit in the audience at one of the debates. Not only was he not invited to it, but he got arrested for having a ticket and sitting in the audience. It is kind of funny that those debates were financed by Anheuser-Bush and Philip Morris. Those really set the political gender for us.

WH: Could you name those six corporations you are talking about?

PD: It is a big mess but you have the whole Rupert-Murdock empire which is NewsCorp, Fox, and several dozen papers. You have the Disney conglomerate which is ABC, Cap City, a bunch of cable stations, and some publishers. You have Time Warner which is now an AOL conglomerate. Those are the big major players, and some of the other networks fall out of part of these big conglomerate companies so, it all comes down to a small set of people.

Let me tell you the political power they wield. In America, it used to be illegal for foreign nationals to own television stations but that changed 6-8 years ago when Rupert Murdock bought Fox network. He had to have an act of congress to accomplish that! At the same time, this congress passed an act allowing a foreign national to own a U. S. television station. The speaker of the house at the time, Newt Gingrich, just happened to sign a 2 million dollar book deal with one of Murdock's publishing companies. I am not saying there is any kind of conflict of interest there, but it sure is suspicious that the government works along those lines.

The same thing happened in China. Rupert Murdock was very anti-communist, but all of a sudden when he wanted to bring his satellite network into China, the premiers daughter gets a $1,000,000 book deal from his network, and he said, "We will bring in television, but we won't bring in any foreign news so you won't have to listen to any anti-communist stuff!"

It is very scary, what is happening in our culture.

WH: An unfortunate thing in life I have found, is..... if you look under the surface, it always comes down to the money.

PD: Our media system certainly comes down to money, and that is what worries me. Children learn this message very quickly. In all the schools I go to, they wear uniforms. They have "Tommy" and "Nike" written on their clothing. When I ask them if they get paid to be a billboard, they look at me like I am stupid! It is really quite scary how we have created a whole culture that worships these things!

WH: Let's talk about the media and why it needs to be changed. Can you give us some specific examples of how the media is brainwashing us?

PD: I think tobacco is the best example here. If you use tobacco as promised, as directed on the package, it will kill you. We know that, yet for years, it has been marketed to children. Tobacco companies claim it is not them doing it, but now that we see the smoking gun in their hands.....and the hands of the movie studios, who are marketing violent movies to children as well. They are claiming it is their first amendment right to sell this poison to kids. That is the argument they have been making, that it is their right to manipulate children into addictive and violent behavior. This is really quite scary.

About four years ago, ABC ran a story saying that Philip Morris spikes the level of nicotine in their cigarettes and that they actually manipulate how much nicotine they put in their cigarettes. This is true. Philip Morris threatened to sue ABC for 16 billion dollars.....but then they did something even worse...... they said they were going to take all their Kraft advertising off the network. The very next day ABC news runs a story apologizing for telling the truth. They would have lost their ad revenues. This is a very clear example of how it works. As long as these advertising dollars flow, we will not get legitimate reports about our products and our culture.

WH: There are some advertisements on television from time to time that use subliminal messages.....both audio and video..... to sell their products. Can you tell us about that?

PD: There is a lot of subliminal nudity that shows up on one

frame where a woman will flash you. Television is a series
of moving pictures. If there are dirty pictures and dirty
frames every second, the conscious mind needs to see about
eight of them before it knows something is there. Yet
television is cut so fast these days that we see a lot of stuff
we don't consciously know it is there, but we are getting a
physical response and these images are impacting us!

Studies have shown that a single frame of nudity can cause
a man's pupils to double in size. This is taking place more
and more, and there is a problem not just with subliminal
messages but the speed the media is moving with quick
cutting, especially for young kids.

Attention Deficit Disorder is skyrocketing in this country and
that is why we have groups like the American Academy of
Pediatrics with 55,000 doctors working with our children and
saying.......no television below age three including computers
and video games. Between the ages of 3 and 7, no more
than one to two hours a day because it affects the child's
development.

Our mass media, instead of telling us about this, are running
commercials about how great they are for kids and how they
take care of them and sell them all kinds of wonderful things.
It is really scary how quick-cut editing is leaning toward a
whole generation that is has less cognitive abilities. Test
scores are dropping wildly in our school systems and we
keep blaming the schools instead of blaming the culture.

WH: What recommendation would you have for the average
person growing up in today's society with respect to the

amount of time they spend on this portion of their life?

PD: The average teenager has a full-time job consuming media. Right now a child spends up to 38.5 hours per week consuming media. That is more time than they spend in school. In fact, for every nine hours a child spends in the classroom, that child will spend about fifteen hours watching television. So, the real teachers are not our schools anymore!

I have to say, it has got to come from the parents...... the kids are going to say, "you can't take this away from me!" Although.....there was this one second-grader who took part in a television turn-off week. He said he hated it, but said he felt better and got better grades as a result! Kids are not going to stop voluntarily, but my recommendations to parents are quite clear. I would like to direct them to my web site at: www.medialiteracy.net I have a whole article on parenting which lists these recommendations.

Limit your children's access to television, watch television with your kids, and talk about what is going on. Put the television in a central location, not in a child's bedroom! If you don't like what you see, turn the stuff off! Parents and adults will say they need the TV to relax, but the reality is that people who are depressed, study after study shows, that they tend to consume a lot of media and television. People who consume little or no television or media are happier.

Is it really making you happy to consume this stuff?
It can't come in if you don't invite it!

WH: I think children pick up on their parents' hypocrasy very readily. It doesn't make any sense to tell your children that television is not good for them and that they should limit the amount of time they spend watching it, if the parents plop down in front of the television themselves and stay there until they go to bed.

PD: You can't just talk the talk......you have to walk the walk!

Television out of the bedrooms means out of the parents bedrooms as well! There are some new products out that are really interesting. I don't want to blast television because I like it. I enjoy the stuff, really, but I understand the trade-off, the price I pay.

The average adult will spend ten solid years watching television before they die and that is without sleep. If God were to show up and say, "Hey, I am going to give you ten extra years to live," that would be a miracle, but how many people would say they would spend it watching television? However that is exactly what we do!

Let me tell you about some new, interesting products. They've got the PDE......Philips Digital Element and it lets you digitally record several hours of television at a time, and with the touch of a button, jump ahead in 30 second increments. All of a sudden, you could eliminate commercials from your life if you wanted to! I think that is an interesting use of technology. The whole rest of the world thinks it is crazy that our stories are told in 8 minute segments with 3 minute commercial breaks in between. The rest of the world tells their stories before they get commercials.

WH: As we said before, it all gets down to money, doesn't it?

PD: Yes! The way our media system is....but it wasn't always that way. When they first had the FTC communications act of 1934, it basically said the public owned the air waves, and television and radio were there to serve the public.....but that all changed in 1996 with the telecommunications act which none of the major networks bothered to report on.

There has been a lot of supreme court decisions down the line which were split in the early days on whether or not these mediums should be commercial or not, and one vote changed that!

A lot of people who understand that making money is all well and good.....and I support that.....but the price is selling a culture of compulsion and addiction. The average child will see a half a million commercials by the age of 18. Almost every one of them would tell that child how bad they are because they don't own this thing or have that certain product. It's the opposite of therapy. It is like saying, "you stink" a half a million times. It's ingrained into our children with powerful graphics and videos.

What price is too high for our soul? How much do we have to sell ourselves before there is nothing left?
WH: Exactly right!
I was reviewing one of the pages on your web site, and Robert, one of the eleventh grade students said, "I love your presentation for tobacco. It made me quit smoking. It has

now been a week after smoking a pack a day for two and a half years. Thanks for saving my life!" What did you tell Robert in that presentation that made him want to stop smoking?

PD: It touches my heart that you bring that up because I get letters like that from students all the time! I basically show them how they are manipulated. I don't tell kids the stuff is bad for them and it is going to hurt them. Rather I say, "Do you like being told what to do? Do you like people lying to you? Here is a whole industry that tells you what to do and lies to you! I go through the ads and show them how the Marlboro men are all dead or have lung disease. I show how the Winston man had a stroke and now goes around telling people how R. J. Reynolds told him it was his job to recruit 5,000 new kids per day. They don't smoke the stuff but the reserve the right to sell cigarettes to the young, the poor, the black, the stupid. They say, "This is what the industry thinks of you!" Here's how their ads show you this! Here is what the ads don't show you. I take children's natural ability to rebel, and redirect it towards people selling them addictive lifestyles. It just gets them riled!

About half the students with whom I work, are up in arms when I leave. Teachers tell me that the best days of school are *after* I come because the kids are so angry!

WH: David, a twelfth-grade student said, "I had never realized just how much energy is put into each and every one of the millions of ads that bombard us each day or how little truism actually exists in the ad industry. When I saw the Anheuser-Bush commercial, the one that says, "Don't drink when you are young, we will wait for your business, I thought they really meant it, but now I am not so sure.

Are the alcohol people trying to get kids to start drinking early?

PD: Absolutely! It is very clear what is going on there! Right now, underage drinking costs our society 52.8 billion dollars a year in suicide attempts, teenage car crashes, depression, and things like that. For a child who drinks any alcohol below age 15, four out of ten go on to become alcoholics. There's a lot of research showing that the younger the children are when they start to drink, the deeper and stronger their addiction becomes. Yet, we have companies that systematically market to them. We have the Budweiser frogs......where there is an older person with a young person together and the older person is telling the younger one to pay attention and obey the rules. The younger person says he doesn't have to and ends up with a Budweiser.

Even though politicians tell us we need more family values, we have a whole media system, particularly the alcohol industry, telling kids to rebel against people who are telling you not to do this stuff and then they use a cartoon character to demonstrate the products. They have ads where people are hiding constantly from family members so they can drink and are giving them a message that they don't have to hide to drink! They have commercials where they joke about people stealing in order to get their beer. They make it very clear.....behaviors of alcoholism, particularly to young people who don't have access or resources to buy, who have to hide in order to drink. That is the theme all their commercials follow.

WH: Is your program of taking a teenager's natural ability to rebel, a means to try to get them to understand what is going on, and to do something about it?

PD: Absolutely! I take their tendency to rebel and say, "Hey! I encourage you to be a rebel. Here is a whole industry that is manipulating you, what are you going to do about it? Are you going to pay extra to put their name on your shirts to be a good fashion person or are you going to say you want to be in charge of your life and make your own decisions. A lot of kids say they are just rebelling and doing for themselves.......but are they really just doing for themselves, or are they doing it for some company that is making money off them.

It is like this.......whenever you and I see a television commercial advertisement, who pays for it? The answer is.....we do when we buy products. In a free market system, if you use something, you pay for it, but television doesn't work that way! It comes to you but you pay extra for products whether or not you see those commercials. That is classic communism and the bad news is that advertisers sell off blocks ads to 10,000 television stations, radio stations, newspapers and magazines. I ask you, what do you call it when somebody sells you and you don't get any money for it? The answer is slavery! When I point that out to people, they start to get angry.

WH: It is kind of overwhelming the way that the thing is

working. I think that we have a lot to be concerned about. Are we going to do something about it?

I know you are passionate about what you do, and you are putting in your full time trying to talk to as many people as possible. What can the average guy do?

PD: Huxley said, "We will cry out for that which slays us." We ask to be slain because we believe it is entertainment. What we need is to shift, and it is going to happen at a lot of different levels. I work with a lot of organizations that train people.... activists of all sorts. I have probably trained three or four thousand people to go out and carry the Media Literacy message.......teachers, doctors, health professionals, citizens, and activists. We are going to need a revolution where we claim back our media system, where we say, "We have rights and this is the public's space All the billboards creeping up and attacking me, all these phone calls into my home, all this direct mail, this is public space." We have the right to have the public space be something more than just an advertisement. That will happen in small numbers at first but it will grow because universally, people resonate with this message. They know something is not quite right. They are feeling more and more depressed and disassociated with their lives. More and more people are taking Prozac. They know that our whole culture is not working for us and so the revolution is going to start small with parents and teachers, but it is going to spread out soon and politicians and other people on the payroll are going to catch up!

WH: You have to ask your self, why is it that such a large percentage of our population is not happy with their life? I have been working with this problem for years. I found the answer in the course of talking with people......they don't have a mission or purpose in their life, something overriding the normal considerations of the day. Therefore, they don't feel motivated to get up every morning and do something and point toward something. They drift into whatever externals people tell them that they need to be doing to make them feel better about themselves. Quite often, the things they do are things that are common and available such a cigarettes, alcohol, relationships with people. You can go on an on with the list of things that people do to try to fix themselves and try to make themselves feel better, but I believe that the answer to this is, you have to have a mission or a purpose.

PD: I agree with you entirely! What I am concerned with is our media system on a whole scale doesn't teach us any of that. It teaches us that our purpose is to consume, to have those junkie consumer goods, and to be in debt.

There is no greater part to your community. Many of us are isolated. We don't know our neighbors, our whole families, our children are in separate rooms watching television away from the parents. Everybody has their own isolated source and they are not being taught how to be connected. They are not being taught they are here for a reason.

There is a spiritual aspect to what I do. The Bible is pretty clear in that it talks about false images and things that really destroy the spiritual message God has for us. And yet, we have a whole culture, a whole entertainment system that is devoted to images that have nothing to do with reality.

WH: How would you define your mission in life right now?

PD: My mission in life right now is wanting to do all the internal work that I need to do and to make sure that I'm in touch with my higher power.....that I am listening to His guidance.....that I need to get to where I make sure I am doing the best I possibly can do for myself and my soul. Once I do that, and as I do that, I know that I can then carry that message.   My message is to work with as many people as I can to say, "Hey, do you want to take control of your life?   Do you want to be the person in charge of your life or do you want to be sold a false bill of good from somebody else who is keeping you a slave and keeping you poor because you think that's the best you can get?"

My mission is to carry the message of a cultural revolution and explain that each of us has a place and the power.   It is time for us to get in tune with our source, and to exercise that power in the community. That enhances all of us.

WH: I certainly salute you in the effort you are making.   I can't think of many things that are more valuable to the individual or to society in general than what you are doing right now.   I also think you have a great message to tell people......that if they are passionate about something in their life, they are not going to be drawn away or diverted by all these things the media is trying to use to divert them into consumerism.

PD: I'm not saying there is anything wrong with having a comfortable house or living a comfortable lifestyle, but I want to know all the trade-offs I am making.   What is the price my soul pays for doing this? Then I can make choices that enhance myself, my community, and the planet. I wake up every morning and I just chuckle! I can't believe God has blessed me to the point where I have a life where I get paid to share the things I am passionate about.

My income is derived from just being passionate. A lot of times when I am in school, I carry that message with me, which is, do what your heart tells you, do what you believe, do what you know is right, and you will be taken care of.

WH: Thank you Peter, we have enjoyed talking with you today.

PD: My pleasure!

Share Your Mission: Volume #2

Patch Adams

WH: Did you happen to see the movie, *Patch Adams* back n December of 1998 or sometime thereafter? Robin Williams portrayed Dr. Adams in a very touching and moving story, a movie that generated a lot of talk at the time. Many people were concerned and interested.......does Patch Adams really exist or was this just made up?

Today we're going to find out the answer to that question because on the end of the line, we have Dr. Adams. Patch, how are you doing?

PA: I'm having the best day of my life.

WH: That's absolutely wonderful. I understand that you're one of the few people who can say that, for the last X number of years, maybe thirty years in your case, you've been doing exactly what you wanted to do in life.

PA: That's true, and I say that wishing it were not unique. I think everyone can follow their dreams.

WH: I have found from practicing addiction medicine for many, many years that people who don't have a purpose in life, who don't have a dream that they're following, tend to get distracted......pulled away by things in the outside environment.....drugs, people, overeating, and many more.......but people who have a dream, something that they are living for do not get distracted. Do you find that to be the case?

PA: I think that having meaning in peoples' lives is a very significant thing to have. Unfortunately, we live in a society whose gods are money and power and in that kind of context, the impression that a child gets is that the important dreams are ones of acquiring both money and power.

No one warns them that they are hollow definitions of success. So they become goals but they're actually not a true thing.....so they never really have an end point to them......except for obtaining more and more. There's a blanket sense of powerlessness all across the nation, a feeling that a person can't accomplish the love that he or she wants, or the individual efforts for their own interests that they want, or the interests that they might have in doing good in the world.

WH: I think that serving other people can quite possibly be the thing that makes you the happiest, regardless of whatever else you have in your life.

PA: I would certainly say that's true in my life and true as a physician. I've seen a few adults that are happy. In some way they were doing something that seemed to be helping others.

WH: You founded the *Gesunheit Institute.* Will you tell us about what that is, what you want to accomplish, where you're at right now, and where you're going?

PA: When I entered medical school, thirty-two years ago, I entered with the idea of using medicine as a vehicle for social change. I'm really a political activist, and so when I entered medical school, I thought that I would study the history of health care delivery with the idea that I would hope to create a model, when I graduated, that addressed every single problem of care delivery.

What that meant is.....when I graduated in 1971, twenty adults, three physicians, and our children, moved into a large six bedroom house and we called ourselves a hospital. We were open twenty-four hours a day, seven days a week for all manner of medical problems from birth to death. We ran this pilot for twelve years until 1983. In that time, we saw 15,000 people to the tune of 500 to 1,000 people a month with from 5 to 50 overnight guests a night.

It was a most intense, wonderful, chaotic, crazy time. In the whole 29 years of our project, we've never charged money for anything that we've done. It wasn't that we wanted to be free for poor people. We wanted to eliminate the idea that one owed money in the medical interaction because we're a political act to recreate community and we cannot conceive of a community of our design that didn't care.......not out of responsibility or guilt for its citizens, but out of the ecstatic delight that one can help their fellow man.

In that same vein we've never accepted any kind of third party reimbursement. We don't feel that Medicaid, Medicare, and Blue Cross, are good organizations. They don't seen to really be what one might hope them to be, and so we have nothing to do with insurance. We've also never carried malpractice insurance. We think that if you carry malpractice insurance you're telling your patients you're afraid of them and don't trust them. We're not going to do that with ours.

We're into the politics of vulnerability. We don't want any protection from people. Also, as family doctors, we realize that people need a lot of time. They want somebody who will get to know them and so our initial interviews with patients are three or four hours long. The idea being that our ideal patient is somebody who wants a deep intimate friendship with us for life. We know with that kind of intimacy that great medicine can happen particularly at a death bed or during intractable pain or chronic illness.

The true reward in the medical life is the reward of intimacy with other people. When we spent that kind of time with people we realized that the vast majority of Americans didn't have a clue about living a vital life. They didn't wake up in the morning ecstatic and thrilled to be alive. It was often in fact, the other way around. So what did it matter if we corrected a blood sugar or a blood pressure if their life was still horrible?

That's why we fully integrated medicine with the performing arts, arts and crafts, agriculture and nature, education, recreation, and social service...... not as acute additions to pharmacy and surgery.....but as the very core of what being healthy is all about. We were interested in not so much normal lab values, as in our patients feeling that they were living the life that they wanted to live, full of friendship, wonder, and curiosity, and a sense of who they wanted to be.

WH: I think that you defined friendship as one of the greatest gifts that a person can give. How would you respond to the question, what is a friend?

PA: In my book, I call it the post-surrender relationship. In a way, since my spiritual base is very worldly, when I hear the term "God" used and hear a truly faithful person talk about their god, I hear them use the words that I think of when I think of friend. So I've grown to think that my metaphor for God is friend. I think the same is true with a faith in one's God or a faith in one's friendship, that they surrender to the deep abiding love that they have with that person.

In my experience as a human for 54 years, there's no question in my mind that the thing that people cherish the most in their lives are their friends. The things that they need the most are their friends and that the worst disease that a family doctor can ever see is the disease of loneliness. Everything that I've accomplished has been on the shoulder of friends.

WH: Back when you were a teenager, you were unhappy, despondent, and you even were admitted to a mental institution. At that time, did you have a purpose for your life, or did it come later?

PA: Well it's interesting. I grew up a very happy child. I had a fabulous mother who gave me self esteem. As I grew up, I was a very good student and my life was happy-go-lucky. Then my father died as a result of war when

I was 16, and that broke my heart. We'd grown up overseas on Army bases and after he died, we had to come back to America. We came back to the south. This was 1961. We became right away embroiled in the civil rights movement.

I felt the pain of injustice and got involved in the civil rights movement and was beaten up frequently. It really hurt me. My father had died as a result of the worst act that a human commits....war...and injustice seemed to be the first cousin to that.

Although my mom gave me a great and happy childhood, she didn't protect me from the adult world. I didn't want to live in a society that celebrated war and racism to the degree that it seemed to. Actually it's funny........I wasn't depressed about me. I was depressed about a world that was so mean to each other and so unkind. I didn't want to live in that kind of a world.

I was in the mental hospital at the age of 18. I did a lot of soul searching and I made two decisions in that hospital that I decided I would do the rest of my life.

One was to serve humanity, and the other was to never have another bad day. I've lived those two intentions now pretty much every day for 36 years and I haven't been sick in those 36 years. I feel, at least for me, that by making a decision to live a happy life and to give to others that it's made my health and my life.

WH: I believe you're right, and I believe that we can take

your experience and extrapolate it to just about anybody. If people can change their attitude and have an attitude of giving in their life, they can be happy, and they don't have to be depressed, have anxiety, or any of the other kinds of psychological problems that most people are caught up with.

You say that people live in their own concentration camp. Please tell us what you mean by that.

PA: In my experience as a family doctor, spending all that time with each individual patient, it seems that when I hear them speak, I hear them lock the doors away from their own happiness. The person that used to play music stopped playing music. The person that used to have faith in something, stopped having faith in that something. The person who had a lover early on was hurt and so they never let themselves have a lover again. Somehow they closed the doors to wonder and curiosity and passion and hope. That becomes their own concentration camp or prison. One doesn't need to have any guards at the doors.

They themselves are self-deprecating. They don't have self-esteem. They don't have a sense of purpose, and society is suggesting to them a kind of purpose that is superficial and hollow.

It's so interesting to me. In our schools we get a huge amount of hours in math and science and history and English, but no one ever gives a class on friendship. No one ever gives a class on faith or wonder or curiosity. No one ever really gets a class on being alive, being vital, following your dreams, or having a vision. If I had something to do with the schools, those would be the kinds of classes I'd make sure they took along with the rest of the things they've been used to teaching.

WH: You said that you're trying to stamp out society's romance and addiction to suffering. Why is there so much negative thinking in this country?

PA: My own theory about it is that we've had in our civilization a romance with pain and suffering since the beginning of recorded time, that is if you look at our history from the beginning, the Greeks, for example, wrote their histories based on men's wars and men's power intrigues. If you look at our religions, however, you will notice in Buddhism and in Christianity, the idea that life is suffering and somehow you have to learn to cope with that. In the modern era, the entire news service all over the world is based on the celebration of suffering. There's never been a single daily newspaper in the world devoted to good news. It's funny. To be more correct, they should say this is the New York Time *Bad* News or the Washington Post *Bad* News. All the news programs are based on bad news and people love it. They lap it up. They can't wait to see another horrible murder on the screen or a disaster that destroys countless numbers. They should warn the young people or all people watching TV that it's bad news and that they're consciously editing out any good news.

Far more good news happens in the world every day than bad news. It's just that between the media and the people that watch TV or buy newspapers, that's how they want to look at things.

If you look at the literature, the visual arts, or the musical arts right now, it's full of bad news. I'm a really big reader, and I challenge groups all over the world to point out five writers of the 20th century whose body of work is about the celebration of life. There's no poetry, drama, or fiction. I haven't found a single person that can come up with five names in the whole world. We're talking about millions of writers. So children grow up and they see their parents grumpy and they hear their parents say, you can't trust strangers, which means six billion people. They tell them, you're lucky to have one or two friends when they should be saying, you're lucky to have one or two thousand. They tell you to lock your door. They see a kind of suspicion and alienation all around them. On top of all of it, they say that one defines success as money and power.

WH: It seems like the priorities are turned way upside down. You believe in the celebration of life and having fun. You've been a clown for years and years. How does making other people laugh and doing your clowning help, with their physical problems, their emotional distress, or their whole aspect of life?

PA: Well clowning brings along with it a huge amount of humor, love, joy, and intimacy. It's a very in-your-face kind of experience. Anything that brings humor, love, or joy so close to it is going to give great relief. It's a great pain reliever of all the kinds of pain, whether it's psychic,

149

spiritual, mental, or physical pain. I've seen it work miracles for 36 years. The pain of the drudgery that most people feel about their life in their hard day at the office, the rough commute home, or another shopping day goes through their heads. The clown throws them a little curve ball and reminds them that there's something else.

WH: A lot of doctors who believe in a more holistic approach to medicine......a mind-body-soul type of relationship, believe that laughter and having fun can really turn around disease processes. You believe in a holistic concept don't you?

PA: I do. Holistic is a word that doesn't have a clear definition in our society. In a way, it's one of those things where you have to know what the person is meaning by that.

WH: Actually, I'm talking about using every type of healing.

PA: Yes, I'm certainly interested in anything that can help relieve suffering or help a person grow. That has a lot of meaning for me. For 30 years, I've been involved in acupuncture, homeopathy, natur-opathy, chiropractic, ayurveda, anthroprosophic, faith healing, herbal medicine, and body work. They're all tools like obstetrics, surgery, and dermatology.

WH: I believe that someone has said that you have somewhere around 15,000 books. In those books, do you remember one that talked about a psychiatrist named Victor Frankle?

PA: Yes. Actually it's closer to 12,000 books. The one you are referring to is *A Man's Search for Meaning.* Victor Frankle was a Jewish psychotherapist who survived the Nazi concentration camps and the only quote of his I know by heart is the one that says, "We who lived in the camps, remember the people who walked through the huts comforting others, giving away their last crust of bread. Though they were few in number, they offered sufficient proof that everything can be taken away from a man, but one thing.....the last of the great human freedoms, the ability to choose one's own way."

WH: Yes, I thought that statement was so dramatic and striking that it's something that I will never forget.

There's only one thing you can actually control in life, and that's your attitude.

PA: I think that's what the Italian movie, *Life is Beautiful,* is all about.

WH: Patch, some people would describe you as revolutionary. Revolutionary in the sense that you would like to change things in our society. What would be the one thing that you would like to see changed if you could wave a magic wand and make it happen?

PA: If I was thinking of the short term, I would wave the magic wand and get rid of all weapons every single weapon on the planet and the ability to make more weapons.

In the long term, because people would just end up making more weapons, I think if we didn't get rid of the systems that we were in, I would have us get rid of the capitalist system where profit, the purpose of which is to make more profit in a world where that system has the made the richest 360 people have the same amount of money as the poorest 2.4 billion.

We live in a society where that's possible, but people that bounce and throw balls are millionaires, and school teachers make nothing. What could be a greater statement for our eventual extinction, that we pay our school teachers nothing and our mere entertainments millions of dollars. It all has to do with economics and greed. Greed has just destroyed our society. We live in the richest country of the world and 80 million people can't get the health care they need.

I've been calling people like Michael Jordan and Bill Gates war criminals publicly, because of the quantity of money that they have, and what they did to get it. Whoever dies tonight of starvation is on their conscience. I hope they feel it's on their shoulders.

I guess if I had to even be more abstract, I'd say the magic wand would say whatever place money and power now have in the world society, I would like replaced by compassion and generosity.

WH: That's certainly an idea that I can identify with. It's something that would be wonderful if it could happen, but I see greed as another one of these addictions that people get into, and just as it's hard to give up cigarettes, it's hard to give up greed. It's probably something that's going to be around with us for a long, long, time unfortunately.

*You've written two books.   One of them is **Gesundheit**. Would you tell us about that?*

PA: ***Gesundheit*** is a book that Universal bought to make the movie about.   It came out in 1993 about our history and philosophy of care and about our plans for our fantasy hospital.   It's also about living a healthy life.

WH: And ***House Calls***?

PA: The other book, ***House Calls***, came out first as a response to noticing that people who came to visit patients in the hospital didn't really know best how to maximize the situation of love.   So I encouraged them to go and become the doctor that used to make the house call themselves and how they can go in a patient's room and instead of being nervous and not knowing what to do, to give them some tools of what to do.   And then I thought about it longer, and I thought gee, however we treat a person on a house call, why don't we treat all people in the world like that?

So I made the book with my favorite cartoonist in history, Jerry Van Amerongin, which is a great honor for me.   I've been a scholar of cartoons, and I don't think there's anybody better in the history of cartoons for really understanding humanity to the degree that he does, and how to celebrate our imperfections and our little differences.   I'm really tickled and I think that I've had a lot of patients and people dealing with patients say it's been useful for them to look at being well and how to make it fun when you're not well.

WH: If our listeners would like to get a copy of these books, how would they go about that?

PA: If they're in the modern age, they can get them at www.amazon.com. They can order them from their bookstore. One is called **Gesundheit** and the other is called **House Calls**. That would probably be the easiest way. I know a lot of bookstores carry one or both of them.

WH: What's the situation with the institute up there in West Virginia now? What do you have built and where are you going with it?

PA: For the first 28 years of our existence, our project was so radical to people that we were unable even working around the clock to get the funds for the only model in America which addressed fully the problems of health care delivery. But thanks to pop culture and its rewards, we are breaking ground in spring and we're going to open in three or four years.

WH: So you have a definite goal of three or four years to be open and be able to show the world what your concept of health care delivery can really be like.

Where do you get funding for this if you don't take money from the patients or third party carriers?

PA: We've probably gotten money from most of the countries of the world. Because of the movie, it looks like we're on the threshold of getting huge quantities of money and most of the donors want to remain anonymous. So let's just say, fairies or angels or magic.

WH: So this project's going to be funded by private donations.

PA: Always has been.

WH: That's wonderful. Patch, we're getting close to the end of the time for the show today, but I'd like to ask you if there's anything that you would like to say to our listeners today with respect to your mission in life. What is your mission Patch?

PA: I think if you look at the decisions I made when I left the mental hospital, that's what I would recommend to the audience; to decide to serve humanity and to celebrate life every day, to really live a happy life, full of gratitude, and in that gratitude, help others.

WH: And with that thought, we're going to wrap it up. We've been talking with Dr. Patch Adams and I'm sure that you've learned a lot of interesting things today. Thanks, Patch for being on the program.

PA: Thank you.

Eric Kaplan

WH: We are pleased and fortunate today to have "Dr. Wellness" as our guest.   Dr. Eric Kaplan is the author of ***Lifestyles of the Fit and Famous***.   Perhaps you have read it or heard about it.   This book is a best seller and has been endorsed by numerous people from Donald Trump to Norman Vincent Peale.

Dr. Kaplan is a chiropractic physician who has an interest in alternative ways of health care combining with conventional medicine to form a complete program of health as opposed to sickness.   Dr. Kaplan has been on multiple television and radio shows around the country including ABC, CBS, NBC and Fox Network.   He has been hailed by ***USA Today*** for his work on the President's council on physical fitness.
We are really pleased to have Dr. Kaplan with us today. How are you today, Eric?

EK: Fantastic!

WH: Great!   As you know, this show has to do with mission and I know you have a mission which we are going to be talking about in a few minutes.   Tell us how you got to where you are at today.   Give us your personal history.

EK: I was a teenage boy who was very interested in athletics.   My career was ended prematurely by a knee injury and it started leading me towards the direction of health care. Also, as a child, I had terrible acne which I believe led me

157

toward nutrition. I started learning about nutrition through a book by Adele Davis who was one of the pioneers of vitamin therapy and alternative health care. It was through that module that I began to hear my calling.

In your introduction I read about your mission and the four questions of why people are put on this planet, and I tell my children that is called darma. Each and every one of us has a uniqueness and what we need to do in our lives is to explore our uniqueness because everybody was put on this planet to provide something to the planet. You see, on this planet nothing is ever removed. Things are only replenished. Things are built. You can't break something down unless you build something else up. You can't build something else up unless you break something else down. Those are the laws of physics.

When I listen to your interviews and your work, I think the thing a lot of people try to realize is what is their uniqueness on this planet and how do they find it! That is something people need to do by becoming comfortable with themselves and accepting them- selves as life's miracle. People are always looking outside for miracles, but I think the true miracle is the miracle of life!

WH: Most people don't fully appreciate their value, and they have different degrees of disliking themselves all the way up to self hate. This is expressed by doing things to themselves like smoking cigarettes........which they know is harmful and will kill them. If we could just get people to understand that they are valuable and they have a real purpose for being here and that they don't need to undervalue themselves, so much more would be accomplished. We would have a more creative world, don't you think?

EK: I agree with that! I think, actually, part of the problem is television. What people need to recognize is that the brain is a computer, and we need to pre-program our computer every day! I think it was Augmen Dino that said, "Some people wake up and say, 'good Lord, morning,' and others wake up and say, Lord, good morning!" Our attitude, as Zig Ziegler says, creates our altitude from the time we get out of bed in the morning . The average child in America watches 7.2 hours of television per day. That is almost 1/3 of their day being spent watching television. The average child spends more time in front of a television than they do with their parents!

I think what we need to do is get back to some of the basics of reading. Charles (Tremendous) Jones says, "You will be the same person you are ten years from today except for the people that you meet, the books that you read, and the places that you visit." I think these are important. What television does is it creates a false sense of reality because it creates a utopia type environment, a world free of problems. Then you have soap operas which creates an opposite world which feeds on the negative. It begins with people recognizing that they were put on this planet even if it was just to carry the seed and bare the child of greatness!

We rarely hear about presidents' parents. We don't hear about Bill Clinton's or Abraham Lincoln's parents. We don't realize that the toughness Lincoln's parents went through or the crisis that Lincoln had in his life! Many people don't recognize what he went through. I talk in my book that in 1816 he was a man who was forced from his home. In 1818 his mother died. In 1831 he failed in business. In 1832 he was defeated for state legislature. In 1833 he went bankrupt in business for the second time. In 1834 he was finally elected to state legislature and then the following year his sweetheart died which caused a nervous breakdown. He spent a whole year in bed. In 1840 he was defeated as elector, in 1843 he was defeated for congress and in 1846 he was finally elected to congress, but in 1848 he lost the election. In 1854 he was rejected for the job of land officer. In 1855 he was rejected for senate. In 1856 he was defeated for vice president. In 1858 he was defeated for senate. In 1860 at the age of 60 years old, over twenty-eight years later, he was elected president of the United States.

With all those failures and so few victories, what made him persevere? I believe that Lincoln had a mission! He had a belief in himself. How many people would have gone bankrupt in business twice, had a nervous breakdown, lost their fiancee, got defeated for everything and yet would persevere and become one of the greatest Americans of all time?

What we need to realize is that even if we fall on our faces, we are still falling forward and the road to success is always under construction!

WH: That is great advice. You are never a failure even if

you fail unless you give up! If you give up then that is the failure. Success might just be around the corner, and it might be so close that if you just try one more day you would have it! That is good advice for people to understand.

Getting back to Og Mandino, I met him just before he died and he allowed me to put in my book, *The Four Questions*, his seventeen great ideas for day to day living. These are some really exceptional ideas. If you haven't had an opportunity to read Og's book. I'd like to send you a free copy of *The Four Questions* so that you can find out what Og Mandino thought about a successful life because he was one of the great motivational speakers and thinkers of all times.

I remember when I heard him last speak, he received a 7-minute standing ovation! The man was absolutely gifted as far as being able to relate to people and help them with their lives.

Call us at 865-546-5537 and find out how to get a copy of the book so you can find out about Og Mandino's seventeen ways to live.

EK: I am looking forward to a copy of that book myself!

WH: Okay, I will get you one out! Dr. Kaplan, I want to ask you about success. People define success in different ways. Some people define it as money, some people as mission. What do you think about success?

EK: It is very funny. I was at a party recently at Donald Trump's estate in Florida.....Moriago..... and I was sitting with a group, and they were asking how much money do you need to be successful? These people were talking to others that had so many zeros, Dr. Henderson, that I was flabbergasted! I think they were startled because when it came to me, I didn't give a numeric answer. I said, "To me, success is being able to do what you want, when you want, with whom you want, and at any time you want!"

I think it caught them off-guard because that is what true success is! There are only so many hours in the day. When we can find something that we love to do and we do that on a day-to-day basis, and we have the opinion that if a person who likes working on a farm ......if you put that person on Wall Street, it is not a matter of money, the person is not going to be happy! Conversely, if you take a gentleman from Wall Street and you put him on a farm and give him a raise, he is probably not going to be happy! I think success is having control of your destiny!

WH: That is exactly the way I think about it! I like what I am doing so much that it would not make any difference even if I had to pay to do it! If the listeners have something they think is important in their lives, that they need to accomplish, and they really enjoy doing, even if they haven't done it yet, they should think about taking that courageous first step because only in following your mission, are you going to be truly happy in life, and only in doing your mission are you going to be truly healthy in life both physically and psychologically!

Your book, ***Lifestyles of the Fit and Famous***, is an excellent book! I just finished reading it and I would like you to tell our audience today a little bit more about the book.

EK: The book is a user-friendly guide to comprehensive health care! Jerry Seinfeld said it best in his best-selling book, ***Sign Language.*** He said, "Everybody wants to be healthy! The amazing thing is, nobody knows where to begin!" What I try to do in my book which was originally published in 1995, is to create a user friendly model that can teach people a proactive way to their health......something they can follow. It wasn't my way or the highway approach! I offered them an empirical formula to the guides and the principles of positive mental attitude, of weight loss, and of vitamins.

Last year in our country there were 45,000 deaths due to automobile accidents and there were 100,000 deaths due to doctor induced disease. Too many drugs that people were prescribed actually made them sicker!

According to Harvard University, conventional care is now the fourth leading cause of death in our country behind cancer, heart disease, and stroke. People have to recognize that all four of these areas are preventable! We know that there are supplements people can take that offset cancer. We know that there are supplements that offset heart disease. We know that there are supplements that can reduce the risk of stroke. And yet, these things are getting little to no recognition!

Last year in our country, $1.7 billion was spent on the antidepressant Prozac alone. It is estimated that one out of five children in our country next year will be on Ritlin or some form of this attention deficit disorder drug. Now they are putting a lot of children on these sorts of antidepressant drugs which are a type of speed drug. They are being resold to other students because of the "speed" quality.

In our country 61,000 people have drug-induced Parkinson's Disease. Julianne Whitaker wrote that 41,000 are hospitalized for ulcers by drugs and 32,000 hip fractures come from falls from drugs. The numbers are staggering. Last year in this country we had 117,000 hospitalizations from anti-inflammatory drugs like aspirin and 17,000 deaths.

People don't realize that Linus Pauling won a Nobel Prize for Vitamin C. Vitamin C has a greater chance of reducing the risk of heart disease and high blood pressure than probably an aspirin a day does and with less side affects.

When we start to utilize common pharmacology as alternative health care, when people will say to take an aspirin a day to reduce heart disease, you are not realizing that aspirin is made up of acetylsalicylic acid and there is a problem.

We have a country whose health care budget last year exceeded a trillion dollars. President Clinton and his wife tried to create a platform on their original election that she was going to set the model to change the formula of health care in our country. She totally failed! Yet, as she is running for senator of the state of New York, it is not even mentioned that she made no changes in health care!

I have had the opportunity to work with the chairman of the President's Council, the honorable Thomas McMillan, and I have worked with the last two Surgeon Generals of the United States. As a result of this work, I realized that there is a major problem in our country and that is my goal, to try to bridge the gap between the east and the west of medicine!

WH: It certainly is a big job, isn't it?

We are talking today with "Dr. Wellness", Eric Scott Kaplan, who has a book out called *Lifestyles of the Fit and Famous*.

Dr. Kaplan, please tell our listening audience where they can get a copy of that book and tell them about your web site.

EK: They can always visit me on my web site. Patients and other people are always welcome to E-mail me at: drwellness.com. The book is usually available through Barnes and Noble, major books stores, and Amazon.com. Again, they can visit my web site and order it right there. What they will find within the book is a simple formula. It teaches them the proper attitude on what vitamins to take. I teach them about the four aces, and how these four elements can reduce the risk of heart disease, cancer, stroke, and high blood pressure. What I do is that I provide them with a model they can use.

For instance, if a person wanted to lose 10-30 pounds, I can show them how to lose that weight in 10 to 30 days. I try to give the reader a pro-active stance.

What Og Mandino was so special for.....he had a way of piercing your spirit and entering your soul. He was one of the motivating sources in my life. What I tried to do was create a book which was requested. I used to have six clinics in the State of Florida where I treated thousands of patients. They always wanted to know what the secrets were.

Then, I had a wife who, unfortunately, was stricken with cancer. She was diagnosed with colon cancer. We went to Sloan Kettering and basically they gave my wife a life sentence. She was told she had approximately 9 months to live! It made me work harder at my profession. It has now been twenty years. It was a devastating thing. Bad things happen to doctors as well! We go through the same crises that all Americans go through! To have my bride and the mother of my children go through a colostomy and have cancer was devastating, but I found that there were programs in Russia which I talk about in great detail in my book. There are alternative treatments to cancer that are utilized throughout the world. Today, we have the ability to access these. I spent hundreds of hours on the Internet finding out what they are doing for cancer in Russia and Germany. In Germany the Commission E, which is the equivalent to our FDA, did a study that found 28% of all prescriptions in Germany are of natural origin, meaning that the medications are natural. Remember, penicillin came from moldy bread, and the most revolutionary drug for the heart, which was digitalis, came from the herb, foxglove!

I talk in my book about dosages and utilization of many alternative remedies.

My new book which will be forthcoming, is called *Awaken The Wellness Within*, which is a guide of alternative health care from A-Zinc. I teach people that there are herbs in this world like astrologus which they would find under the letter A. Astrolugus is an antiviral agent. We must prepare ourselves because we have an epidemic of viruses.

Over the last few years, not only has there been a movement towards more aids, but we are starting to see resurgence to things like tuberculosis. We see things like flesh-eating bacteria. *Time Magazine* did a cover story that said, "Are we losing the war against infectious disease?" What people have to realize is that they are at war!

If you go into a supermarket, look around. How many foods are infiltrated with drugs and chemicals? Our meats come from animals that are raised with antibiotics in them. We are passing this on to our children.

I talk about simple things like ear infections. Last year in this country, $500,000,000 dollars was spent on ear infections for children. *The New England Journal for Medicine* revealed that children who took amoxicillan had four to six times more recurrent ear infections than those who didn't. Imagine, the *New England Medical Journal,* which is the most respected medical journal around, said that children who took amoxicillan for ear infections had four to six times the rate for recurrent ear infections. Do you realize that this drug is still being prescribed today as we speak, for ear infections?

What I try to do in my books is to let a person know that they can look up any letter in the alphabet and find a symptom and a treatment. We talk about supplements, disease, and treatments by providing an alternative or natural approach first!

WH: As you know, the basis of this program is to help people, through the examples of our guests, to understand, that mission is important in their lives and they are going to only be really truly happy if they have a mission and start pursuing it.

What's your mission?

EK: Henry Ford once said, "You can't build a reputation on what you are going to do." My mission is very simple! I am trying to bridge the gap between conventional and alternative care. I call this complimentary care! I am trying to change the paradigm of health care which is basically a sickness based model to a wellness based model.

I had the opportunity to spend the last five years on Wall Street, running a public company called *Complete Wellness Centers,* where what we did was to bring chiropractors together with medical doctors, physical therapists, and neurologists. We made a major acquisition of a major portion of the weight-loss program, NutriSystem.

When we took over NutriSystem, we brought them away from FenFen and Meridia. We moved them to other mechanisms. My book deals a lot with low carbohydrates and moderate fat principles. This is a kind of a mixture and a merger of the straight direction that Dr. Atkins goes. I believe that there are carbohydrates that people can easily utilize. Greens, salads, fruits, are free carbohydrates. Let people eat them as much as they wish!

My mission is to try and let the patient take control of their life......to try to bridge the gap and let people know that there are natural approaches to health care. There is a wellness based model.

For example, today, where does the average American go if they are not well? They haven't had a heart attack, but they are not well. Do they go to a hospital or to an emergency sickness center? Do they go to a basic medical doctor? Do they go to a health club or a fitness center? Do they go to a chiropractor or a back or neck center?

What I try to do with both my medical doctors and my chiropractors is.....and we did this in a public forum, which was greatly accepted on Wall Street.....is we tried to create a wellness model based on attitude, exercise, nutrition, in which the patient could take control of his or her destiny, and not be led by the illusions of television and advertising.

We are trying to compare ourselves with models on television that are 17 and 18 years old that have never had two, three or four children. They don't have a job that goes from eight in the morning to five at night and then have to come home and feed the children! We are competing with standards that nobody can meet which is why there is such a revolution in plastic surgery today. People are trying to look better, but health and happiness is not something that comes from the outside, it comes from within!

WH: We are talking with Dr. Eric Scott Kaplan today and you can get him at *www.drwellness.com*. For our international listeners, we recommend this way of communicating with Dr. Kaplan. Get a pencil and paper and write down *www.drwellness.com* and you can go from there.

Dr. Kaplan, your final comment.

EK: I think that everybody should remember this: The past is history. Everything that is done is done. The future is a mystery but this moment of life, this moment that we have right now, here today, that is the gift, and that is why we call it the present! Enjoy your present which is your gift of life.

Thank you very much!

WH: Thank you for being on today, Dr. Kaplan. We really appreciated your message!

Paul J. Meyer

WH: We have the privilege today of having Paul J. Meyer as our guest. Mr. Myer is the founder and CEO of Success Motivation Institute, Inc., which was started in 1960. SMI is to success and personal achievement in life as Coca Cola is to soft drinks or Xerox to photocopiers. Mr. Meyer has authored 24 full-length success and motivation programs over the years to help people develop their true potential in life and have greater success in all aspects.

More important, Paul believes in God and Jesus Christ and how you are able to put your life together successfully as a result of good spiritual principles.

Paul's books and audiotapes have been translated into 24 languages in over 60 countries. Now, from Aspen, Colorado..... Paul J. Meyer. Good Morning Paul!

PJM: Good Morning!

WH: You started off in the insurance business originally, didn't you?

PJM: Yes I did. At the age of nineteen, I started in the insurance business in Georgia.

WH: There are some interesting stories that I read in one of the books about National Union, can you tell us a little bit about that and what you got out of that experience.

PJM: National Union was an insurance company I worked with, and we actually wrote more business than the company could handle. The way the insurance business works, it takes 150 percent of the premiums to put the business on the books. The company had a great deal of financial difficulty because my agency wrote more new business than they could afford to handle....plus the company had poor management. I had a choice when the company was not doing well to either leave and take the commissions that I had earned or stay and help correct this mess.

My attorney then was Alan Clements, an associate of Senator Claude Pepper. I said to Allen, "Well, I would rather do the right thing because it is the right thing to do." He asked, "What is that?" I said, "I would like to help straighten the whole thing out," I did just that, but it took eighteen months and most of my money. The one thing I learned was as Allen pointed out, that if I straightened it out, I would not even get any thanks. But I said I didn't need any thanks.

When it was over, Senator Pepper said I was the richest young man he had ever met. I was 27 at that time, and I asked him what he meant because I was almost broke. He said, "Because of what you have learned at this age and what you know about people, I think God is going to use you in an amazing way." Of course, I didn't fully understand what he meant at the time. Through this experience I learned what God intended for my life. It certainly wasn't the insurance business, for when I prayed and asked God, "What now?" I felt like that door slammed - but another one soon opened.

My pastor told me about Word Records, Inc., which is now Word Publishing, owned by the Thomas Nelson Publishers. Word Records was having difficulties, and my pastor thought I could learn what I was cut out to do while helping the company. I asked, "What's that?"

He replied, "I watched you sell an insurance policy and then stay afterwards to show somebody how to achieve goals that could completely change lives. That is when you turn on, when you are talking to somebody about utilizing God-given potential. That is what you need to do for a career. When I told him I didn't know how to do that, he said, "You can learn about the record business and publishing business from Word and help them get on track --- and then launch your business from there!" That is exactly what I did!

WH: This story that you have been telling us about says a lot about your personal integrity and courage, which is what you do when no one is looking. I am impressed with you and your life and everything that has happened to you.

When you are talking about your God-given mission in life, that is exactly what we're interested in telling people about. If they find out why it is that God created them and they start to pursue that with all the passion that they can develop, they are going to be the happiest people on earth. Do you agree with that?

PJM: Yes, we are all here for a purpose! My mission statement is simple: I plan to do all the good I can by all the means I can, in all the ways I can, in all the places I can, for all the people I can, as long as I can. I am Jesus Christ's bond-servant. I wake up every morning and say, "This is the day the Lord has made, I will rejoice and be glad in it!" My first prayer every morning is, "God, give me somebody to minister to today!"

WH: I wake up each morning thankful for another day... to be able to get just a little closer to my goal and to accomplishing my mission. Every day is another opportunity.

I have found in life that some people who don't have that philosophy or that gratitude get up and are depressed. They don't want to go to work, and they have all kinds of problems. If they would just turn it around and see the other side of things, it would make a difference. Paul, I want to talk about your philosophy of living, for philosophy gives direction, purpose, and force to your mission in life. Your philosophy is based on a pentagon... five different precepts - principles for living from the Scriptures. Please comment on each of them after I have stated them:

One...***Let this mind be in you which was also in Jesus Christ.***

PJM: The reason I start off with this point in my philosophy of living is because I believe that attitude is everything. Attitude is a habit of thought; if you change the way you think, it can improve your life. Most people, because of the way they were conditioned, have a negative attitude. They see the glass as half-empty instead of half - full. I believe every morning that if I could think like Christ today, act like Christ today, love like Christ today, give like Christ today and forgive like Christ today, I am going to have a heck of a day!

WH: Two...***Be anxious for nothing but in everything in prayer and supplication with thanksgiving, let your request be known to God and the peace of God which surpasses all understanding will guard your heart and minds through Christ Jesus!***

PJM: I think it is a sin to worry! Regardless of what happens to us, it is our duty as a Christian to be thankful for it! If we believe that in every adversity is the seed of an equivalent - or greater - benefit, and work for it, we won't worry. I don't have a worry bone in my body! It never crosses my mind to worry about anything because as a

Christian, I don't have to worry - God is in control.

WH: I used to practice general medicine. Twenty-five percent of the people who came to see me, came for the symptoms of anxiety and depression. They wanted pills and other kinds of things to get rid of these symptoms but the only thing that can really get rid of anxiety and depression is a firm foundation on Jesus and God.

PJM: Absolutely!

WH: Three...*Not that I speak in regard to need for I have learned whatever state I am in to be content.*

PJM: My friends say, "How do you feel when you are losing?" I have started 100 companies since I was fifteen, and 65% of them did not work. I tell my friends it is like baseball, you win some and you lose some! I am happy *with* and *without*. That is what the Apostle Paul said in Philippians 4:11 and I have learned to be content with whatever state I am in.

WH: Four... *I can do all things through Christ who strengthens me.*

PJM: Think about that! I have been in marketing all my life and I always laugh when I go in to sell somebody and I think, "Well, what am I here for?" As a Christian, I am always supposed to think more of other people than I do of myself. So I am there to be of service. I am marketing something, and I think, "I've got Jesus Christ as my partner!" Every thing is God's by right of creation, so what ever I do, it is for the advancement of the word of Jesus Christ. No matter what I am doing, I can't have me in control of my life and Christ in control of my life at the same time. It has to be one or the other of us. That was my mother's favorite Scripture and it is one of my favorites.

WH: I certainly believe that. Jesus said, "If you have the faith of a mustard seed, you can move mountains," so when you throw action on top of that, you can do just about anything!

Now, the fifth point of your philosophy is: *Give and it will be given to you, good measure, pressed down, shaken together and running over will be put into your bosom with the same measure which you use, it will be measured back to you.*

PJM: As I said before, everything is God's right by creation. Tithing should just be the start of our giving. That means not just in your church but also helping in any and every possible way you can. If you see someone that needs something and you have the ability to give it, you are supposed to give it! There are 66 books in the Bible, but there is only one place where God challenges us: Malachai 3:10 where he says, "Bring what you have into the storehouse and I will pour you out a blessing where you won't have a place to hold it." This Scripture is a financial stewardship message. I do a lot of counseling with people who have financial problems and want me to help them financially. I use Biblical principles and agree to help them under the condition that they give ten percent of their next check to their church or to a charity. They often say, "Well, I can't pay my bills now!" I tell them that I can't do much myself, but with God and the Holy Spirit working with me I can do wonders. But we can't get into the loop unless we make a sacrificial gift and that has to be on the front end of the money -- not the back end. If you are going to give what is left over, you haven't given anything! You must give out of the first money you get. I have five children - all Christians - and they give on the front end of their money . They live off what is left and that is what I try to communicate to all our employees, our clients, and others. I tell about ste·.·ardship because the Scriptures are quite clear that your heart is where your pocketbook is.

I was speaking at St. Andrews University in Scotland at a seminary at St. Mary's where they asked me to speak on, "Can a rich man enter the kingdom of heaven?" I said, "You bet he can, and he can take a whole bunch with him if he does it right! Why don't I challenge all of you right now? Take your checkbooks out and let me walk down each aisle and look to see what you did with your money the last sixty days, and I'll tell you where your heart is!" At first, they flinched but afterwards, of the 50 or so pastors there one said, "I think that message needs to be preached in Scotland because our churches are empty and as lifeless as the Dead Sea!" If you take it all in but don't give any of it out, your life is going to be dead the same way! We need to give our money, our time, and our talent and then we are going to have the joy we are talking about in this philosophy of life outline.

WH: That is a great philosophy! I think if more people would stop and spend some time thinking about that, we would have a lot happier people.

You have written a number of full-length programs - 24 in all, and several books. In addition, several books have been written about you A book that was written about you by John Edmund Haggi is *Paul J. Meyer and The Art of Giving*. Please tell us about that book.

PJM: John Edmund Haggi is the founder of the Haggi Institute, a mission organization based in Atlanta Georgia. This organization goes to third-world countries to find leaders and teach them the skills of evangelism and how to stand on their own two feet financially from a Christian standpoint. Then they are taught to go out and train others to be missionaries. The Haggi Institute has graduated about 35,000 leaders; each has trained an average of 100 others in the third world - where over 50% of the world's population lives.

John spent about 10-12 years trying to get me to let him write a book about me from a stewardship standpoint, and I told him *No!* Finally, after all those years, he convinced me that a book could be used to influence others to be givers. We have had incredible feedback from the book John wrote, and we have used it to influence thousands of people to reconsider their position on giving.

WH: One of our mutual friends, Mark Victor Hansen, co-author of *The Chicken Soup For The Soul* series, said you co-author a book called, *Chicken Soup For The Golden Soul* can you tell us about it?

PJM: I have been friends with Mark Victor Hansen for some time. Dr. Barbara Cheser in our office and I worked with our research group to put together a couple of hundred stories written about or by people 60 or older living purposeful, meaningful lives. By the way, the total Chicken Soup series has now sold over 60 million copies, which is one of the most phenomenal publishing efforts in history!

Chicken Soup for the Golden Soul has to do with seniors. It was a joy working with all the people who contributed stories. I realized when we were collecting stories that it is amazing how everybody has a story and everybody has a story that can be an inspiration to other people! Our book appeared on every major best-seller list. I have encouraged people to write down what has influenced them in their lives, what's their greatest contribution to life, who has influenced them, and who has been their best role model. People need to write this information down so they can share it with their children and their grandchildren.

WH: You're working on a new book, I understand, tentatively entitled, **Unleashing Your Legacy**.

PJM: Yes, one chapter is going to be about integrity and another chapter will be about how we all stand on level ground. I am one of the few people I know about or have met in my life who doesn't have any prejudice. I don't have to agree with what people do or what they think. But we all need to love the Lord our God with all our strength, all our mind, and all our spirit, and love our neighbors as ourselves. Those are the two most important commandments. The second one is what I am talking about in one of the chapters.

Another chapter in my book is, *"My Word Is My Bond."* Years ago, I made so many business deals where I would just shake hands with somebody and say I would see them at the closing. We used our word and nothing else. I have gone around the world to about 60 countries and set up general directors to market the programs I have written. In most cases, we never had a contract but just a handshake, and we never had a disagreement with a single one in forty years.

I think people's word needs to get back to Biblical principles. When you say something, you need to mean it and back it up!

WH: You hit some really important points today. Another point that comes to mind that we haven't talked about was what Christ taught about judgementality... not trying to judge other people because only the person and God know their heart.

PJM: We have no business judging anybody about anything. My mother wouldn't let anybody say anything bad about anybody. If you kept it up, she would leave the room! She said if you can't say something good about them, do not say anything at all!

WH: That is a great philosophy! I would like to ask you about something that is close to your heart: Summers Mill.

PJM: A friend of mine used to own Southfork where the television series *Dallas* was filmed. My friend knew I was interested in getting a farm but I told him I didn't just want a plain piece of ground. I wanted something unusual. He called me one Sunday after church and told me about Summers Mill, which is one of the most photographed places in Texas. One of the last standing mills, it has a 200-foot-waterfall right next to it.

We bought the mill and surrounding land, but I didn't know what to do with it because I am not a farmer. On the Summers Mill land, there is a horse farm which we lease, but on the other side of the highway, I started an ostrich business. Several years ago I sold all the ostriches and decided to turn the farm into a Christian retreat and conference center. I made this decision because my wife said everyone who visited Summers Mill said it was one of the most serene and picturesque places they had ever been.

We took the building where the hatchery was and turned it into a large meeting room, seating about 150 people. We took the building where the chicks were and made it the Big Bird Lodge. It has ten suites with queen-sized beds in each room. We now have the Blue-Bonnet Lodge and the Chisolm Trail Lodge and eight different conference rooms in all. We can sleep about 150 people. Churches within a 200- mile circle who come to Summers Mill Retreat and Conference center. We have women's retreats, men's retreats, and seminars someone like yourself would hold for counseling. These are conducted over the weekends, but during the work week we let businesses use the center.

We have been operating Summers Mill Retreat and Conference Center for only three years and already, fifty percent of our business is repeat business! Seventy five percent of the business is word of mouth! We have had many comments from people accepting Christ while they were at the center. I am overjoyed about how the Lord has blessed this work.

God brought us the most beautiful couple, Bill and Alma Bunting, who run the ministry, and are doing a wonderful job. My wife's sister and her husband take dare of the entire farm. The Conference Center is located on a huge amount of acreage and has a couple of miles on the Salado Creek.

WH: If anyone would like to have more information on Summers Mill Retreat and Conference Center they can go to www.summersmill.com. Where would someone find out more about you and what you are doing? Is there another web site that would be better?

PJM: Yes, other web sites include: www.lksupport.com, www.lmi-inc.com, and www.success-motivation.com.

WH: We have been talking today with Paul J. Meyer about his five-point philosophy of life, how it supports his mission, and some of the ways he is carrying out his mission. He is recognized as a founder of the whole industry of personal success and achievement. He has had a tremendous life and tremendous career, and a great percentage of his success comes from his belief in God and Jesus and the principles in the Bible.

Paul, thank you for being on the program today.

PJM: My pleasure.